A Conspiracy
OF Love

Living Through & Beyond
Childhood Sexual Abuse

Wendy Read

Wendy Read

A Conspiracy OF Love

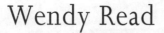

Living Through & Beyond
Childhood Sexual Abuse

Northstone

Editor: James Taylor

Cover design: Margaret Kyle

Interior design: Verena Velten

Proofreader: Dianne Greenslade

NORTHSTONE PUBLISHING is an imprint of WOOD LAKE BOOKS, INC.
Wood Lake Books acknowledges the financial support of the Government of Canada,
through the Book Publishing Industry Development Program (BPIDP) for its publishing activities.

WOOD LAKE BOOKS is an employee-owned company, committed to caring for the environment
and all creation. Wood Lake Books recycles, reuses, and encourages readers to do the same.
Resources are printed on recycled paper and more environmentally
friendly groundwood papers (newsprint), whenever possible.
A percentage of all profit is donated to charitable organizations.

Library and Archives Canada Cataloguing in Publication

Read, Wendy, 1953–

A conspiracy of love: living through & beyond

childhood sexual abuse/Wendy Read.

ISBN 1-896836-77-1

1. Read, Wendy, 1953-. 2. Adult child sexual abuse victims – Religious life.

I. Title.

BV4596.A25R42 2006   248.8'6   C2005-907370-5

Published by Northstone Publishing
an imprint of WOOD LAKE BOOKS, INC.
9590 Jim Bailey Road, Kelowna, BC, Canada, V4V 1R2
250.766.2778
www.northstone.com
www.woodlakebooks.com

Printing 10 9 8 7 6 5 4 3 2 1
Printed in Canada by
Houghton Boston Printers, Saskatchewan

Dedication

This book is dedicated to my sisters and brother
Penny, Jen, Christina, David and Kathy
and to the memory of my sister Mary P. who did not survive.

CONTENTS

Acknowledgments

This book would not have been possible without the encouragement of many people. I would like to thank:

- Lee MacKay, friend and soulmate, who taught me how to articulate both terror and joy.
- Hilary Cashman, whose friendship has helped to set me free to write.
- Marlene Hunter, physician and counselor, for her confidence in my ability to heal.
- Aled Jones Williams, for his Christmas sermon.
- Brian Thorpe, for conversations about his work with former students of residential schools.
- The worshipping communities of Mount Seymour United Church in North Vancouver, BC, and the Victoria (BC) Monthly Meeting of the Religious Society of Friends.
- Friends who provided a supportive space for me to write, or who read excerpts and offered suggestions: Jen Read-Heimerdinger, Ted Bristow, Selma Sheldon, Sheila Norris, Jim McCullum, Marian and Tom Barnett, Christina Dunn, and Joanne Black.
- The FaithTrust Institute in Seattle, WA, and the Cleveland Child and Family Trust in England, for their sponsorship.
- The staff at Wood Lake Books, especially Lois Huey-Heck for her vision and commitment, and Jim Taylor for his patience and advice.
- My children Chris and Thomas, for their consistent support and love.

Foreword BY MARIE M. FORTUNE

The Bible matters to Christians. Whether the Hebrew or Christian texts, we study, we pray, we preach, we reflect in hopes of understanding God's word on this particular page. We do this because we believe that not only is the Bible the story of God's people but that it is our story, too. We sometimes speak of the Bible as the Living Word – not only is it great poetry and literature, but somehow it continues to speak to the contemporary reader. The pilgrim, John Robinson, is quoted as saying: "There is always more light and truth to break forth from the scriptures."

Scripture is a powerful and often ambiguous source of our self-understanding as Christians. Tragically, scripture has too often been misused, resulting in great harm to children and adults who have been abused. For example, it is blasphemous to suggest to a child who is being sexually abused at home that the commandment to "Honor your father and your mother" means to keep silent and never confront the abuse. And yet it is in scripture where we find a critical clarification of this commandment. In Ephesians 6, the writer repeats the commandment to honor one's parents and then adds: "Do not provoke your children to anger but bring them up... in the discipline of the Lord." This is the message that the survivor of childhood sexual abuse needs to hear – the caution to parents to not drive their children to anger, which is what mistreatment and abuse will surely do.

What if our reading and interpretation of scripture were passionate? What if we read and interpreted as if our lives depended on it? What if we really read and interpreted through the lens of experience, including the child's experience of abuse?

Then we would have this act of faith and witness given us by Wendy Read. She has taken powerful texts and answered each one with a psalm. In Hebrew scripture, the psalms are songs of lament, anger, thanksgiving, and joy. These postmodern psalms cry out with rage, grief, love, and healing. Like the psalmist of old, this author does not mince words. In a paraphrase of Jesus' words, "You shall know the truth, and the truth will make you flinch before it sets you free."

Oftentimes it is the unexpected text that reveals profound meaning. For example, the Transfiguration (Mark 9:2–9), Jesus in the garden betrayed by a kiss (Mark 14:44–46), Jesus appearing after the Resurrection (John 20:19–23) – these are texts seldom mentioned when considering sexual abuse. Yet here too we find God still speaking.

The Bible is a resource which should not be denied to those who have lived through sexual abuse. But neither should it be used to hit them over the head. It should never be used to condemn or shun one who has been victimized. Rather the Bible is God's ongoing gift to people of faith, given to be a source of help, support, and understanding in the midst of life's traumas.

Scriptures to accompany one's prayer life, to stimulate one's preaching, to expand one's understanding – all are possible when we look to the scriptures with open eyes, a clear mind, and a willing heart. We need truth-telling, we need grace revealed, we need justice-making, we need the abundant gifts available in the Bible to guide us through the journey to reclaim our faith even as we remember our histories.

Thanks be to God who gives us this gift and to writers like Wendy Read who give us access to it.

Introduction

A Conspiracy of Love is an exploration of scripture, as seen through the lens of childhood sexual abuse, and offers reflections on a variety of biblical passages as a resource for healing. Although it is primarily intended for those who have themselves suffered childhood sexual abuse, it will speak to anyone interested in the intersection of suffering with faith.

Although the reflections were written over a period of three years, they represent closer to 20 years of working to heal from the sexual abuse that I experienced throughout my childhood. I hesitate to say I have "healed," as in "fully recovered." That will never happen, any more than someone who has lost their legs in a terrible car accident is one day going to heal by growing new legs. I use the word healing to talk about a process, rather than a finished product. For me, it has been the process of remembering what happened, understanding the mechanisms by which I coped, and learning to adapt to a non-abusive environment.

The underlying message given by abusers to their victims is that they are worthless, except as objects to be possessed and used by stronger and more powerful people. Certainly this was true for me. Staying alive depended on my participation in the conspiracy of silence that allowed the abuse to continue.

However, at the same time, there were people, places, and circumstances that seemed to work together to counter the message that I was inherently worthless. School was a safe haven, where I was affirmed by teachers and friends. Within cycling distance of home were the North Yorkshire moors where, with siblings, friends, or alone, I found freedom for hours or even days at a time. The essential goodness of life that I glimpsed as a youngster has since been reinforced a hundredfold by close friends, skilled counselors, a strong connection with nature, and my faith. A conspiracy of love has prevailed.

The Christian Church has a unique and essential role to play in healing, alongside secular institutions such as counseling agencies, women's resource centers, and the medical profession. However, in many places the Church has been slow to recognize this; it has been reluctant to address the evil and the injustice inherent in sexual abuse, and slow to reach out with compassion to those who suffer the aftermath of childhood trauma. Some churchgoers who were sexually abused as children often question how the message they hear in church is relevant to the complexity and struggle of their lives. Miraculously, they are still able to draw on their own spirituality for strength to persevere on the long journey towards wholeness.

The gospel that is at the heart of Christianity proclaims freedom to the oppressed and relief to the downtrodden. In the realm of heaven that Jesus spoke about, the vulnerable are befriended, the wounded are healed, and the perpetrators of harm are brought to justice.

It is from this standpoint that I have written the reflections in this book. They show the possibilities for healing when we have the imagination and the courage to let our faith – including the written story of our faith – intercept the profound suffering inherent in childhood sexual abuse. I have drawn on my own childhood experience as well as on personal stories shared with me; where necessary I have changed the details to protect the privacy of others.

Language

Because confusion about the meaning of words often abounds for children growing up in abusive situations, it is important in any conversation pertaining to sexual abuse that we clarify our own use of language.

The word most often used for someone who was sexually abused as a child is "survivor." Many people find this word appropriate. However, for a number of reasons it doesn't work for me, and I rarely use it. On the one hand, survivor can suggest that since I have survived, all is well; I am still alive, so what is my problem? On the other hand, survivor can suggest that

I am completely defined by the grim reality of the violence inflicted on me in childhood; it can prevent people from seeing me primarily as a person with a full range of life experience. I find other words, such as victim or warrior, equally problematic. Instead, when referring to myself or others in the context of sexual abuse, I tend to use a phrase such as "those who have endured childhood sexual abuse." In my writing I do my best not to make this too cumbersome.

"God" is the most common word for the Divine, and – again – many people, especially in churches, find this appropriate. I tend to use the word God only as shorthand, in an academic sense. For me "God" generally denotes a male being, equivalent to "Goddess" which denotes a female being. Both God and Goddess fail to describe adequately the full nature of the Divine. Indeed, all words are inadequate, but I find those words and phrases that emphasize attributes such as life, love, mystery, and holiness without specific reference to gender to be a closer expression of the One I know and relate to as the Divine. However, if a reader is more comfortable with the word God, then I hope that that is what she or he will understand when I use "Holy One" or "Creator" or "Source of Life."

Many Christians have grown up using "Father" as a descriptor for God. At its best this image incorporates attributes of the Divine, such as love and protection. However, some Christians who were abused by their fathers associate Father with punishment rather than protection. It is not then a helpful image in the context of healing. Substituting "Mother" is helpful to some, but again if our mothers were either abusive or failed to protect, this image is also problematic. Jesus used a variety of metaphors, stories, and parables to portray the many different aspects of his Creator. His use of the term Father shows the intimacy of his relationship with God. It is more important to convey the possibility of intimacy that Jesus knew than to insist on using an English translation of his exact words.

The choice of scriptural texts

The scriptural texts that provide the basis for the reflections are from the *Revised Common Lectionary*; they will be familiar to people who participate regularly in lectionary-based worship. Many of the texts will be well known to those with even a limited knowledge of the Bible. Within the scope of the lectionary, I have chosen passages that particularly lend themselves to consideration of truth, evil, suffering, community, healing, forgiveness, and thanksgiving.

Unless otherwise indicated, the scripture passages quoted are taken from the New Revised Standard Version.

How to use this book

This book will be of interest to
- Adults who were sexually abused as children
- Their partners and friends
- Ministers, priests, and pastoral care workers
- Spiritual directors/accompaniers
- Counselors

Because of the nature and intensity of some of the reflections, readers in the process of healing from childhood sexual abuse are advised to have a counselor or close friend available for support.

The four themes of the book are Truth, Community, Life, and Grace. Several reflections are offered for each theme, although this is only a matter of emphasis. The importance of truth, life, community, and grace are evident throughout the book.

The book can be used in a group setting, either by people who were abused and/or by friends and supporters. The material is suitable for both secular and church groups.

The questions at the end of each reflection are intended to guide readers through their own responses to the chosen text and to the author's reflection. One or two of the questions might be sufficient for this purpose. Journaling, group discussion, conversation with a counselor or minister, and prayer, are a few of the ways for readers to articulate their responses.

Part 1

Truth

Ready or not,
here comes the Holy

"But about that day or hour no one knows, neither the angels in heaven, nor the son, but only the Father. Beware, keep alert; for you do not know when the time will come. It is like a man going on a journey, when he leaves home, and puts his slaves in charge, each with his work, and commands the doorkeeper to be on the watch. Therefore, keep awake — for you do not know when the master of the house will come, in the evening, or at midnight, or at cockcrow, or at dawn, or else he may find you asleep when he comes suddenly. And what I say to you, I say to all: Keep awake."

MARK 13:32-37

Reading any passage from the Bible can be treated as an academic exercise in which to ask and debate questions of purpose, author, audience, context, form, allusions, and genre. But even academic exercises are never carried out objectively. No matter who we are, no matter how rigorous our scholarship, we cannot completely set aside our own context, knowledge, beliefs, and experience. We deceive ourselves if we say, "This is the truth of this passage." It is more honest to admit, "This is the truth we find in this passage, today."

The passage from chapter 13 of Mark's gospel (or a parallel passage from one of the other gospels) is traditionally read in churches on the first Sunday in Advent. Often referred to as the Little Apocalypse, it sets aside any illusions that Advent is a sentimental waiting for Christmas, and urges us instead to concern ourselves with being prepared for the coming of the Holy One. On the one hand we have our work to do and our daily routine to follow, yet on the other hand we do well to maintain a constant state of expectation. At any moment, anything might happen.

For those of us who have had to cope with trauma as young children, especially repeated trauma, the language of apocalyptic literature appears to relate to that part of our lives we would prefer not to have lived. There are parallels between the predictable unpredictability that an abused child learns to live with and the promise of the sudden intervention by a mighty power at some unknown future time. "Only the Father [knows when]" applies equally to the End of the World and the end of a day in the life of a young victim of nighttime incest. Traumatized children do not need to be given the instructions, "Keep alert," "Be on the watch," and "Keep awake." We do all that instinctively to preserve for ourselves a few scraps of power, control, and self-determination.

During the process of therapy, which necessarily involves remembering terrifying events and reclaiming intense feelings of helplessness, anger and shame, there is at times a sense of catastrophe. Flashbacks interrupt ordinary daily life. Old ways of coping are judged and discarded to make way for strange new behavior that is difficult to learn. Relationships with family, friends, abusers, and witnesses are radically refashioned once the secrets of long ago are told. Irrational hope drives us on; a thin strand of trust and connection with something holy pulls us into a deeper relationship with love; glimpses of unfamiliar freedom make us both laugh and cry. We wonder if we are going mad.

Afterwards – as much as there is any "afterwards" to healing from events that steal so much of a person from themselves – it is possible to be more aware, more awake to other situations that know disaster and devastation. Gradually, we can choose to see, and speak out, and join in the struggle to overturn other injustices in the world. Our ability to endure, and our willingness to risk transformation and new life, can be used to empower other vulnerable parts of creation.

The following is how I might interpret that apocalyptic text from Mark's gospel, made in light of having been abused both by my father, who was a doctor, and by a priest at our local church.

◇◇◇◇◇

Before the age of words a message was given, through gesture and stillness, silence and sound.

"Little one, helpless and vulnerable in body and mind, I will come again when I choose, without warning, so look out. It might be tonight or it might be after a few more nights. You cannot know, for only I know and I will not tell. I, your physician-father, might come alone or I might come with another, your priest-father from church. You are ours to do with as we will. When we come we will judge you, and if we find you waiting and ready for us we will be pleased. We will have our way with you and take what we want. But, if we find you asleep or hiding from us, we will first remind you that you are ours. Then we will have our way with you and take what we want. So look out, little one! Always be ready for us to take from you what is not your own: your body, your mind, your innocence, your trust."

Before the age of words there was terror screaming in the silence and rage pounding in the night. Before the age of words there was blind trust, mad hope, and utter powerlessness. Far away from this world where evil ruled, my grief-filled spirit fled, to abide in exile with the Holy. There were no words here yet either, only the embrace of my spirit by the Creator of the Universe. The tenderness of love shone in the tears the Creator shed, tears of solidarity, anger, and longing.

Before the age of words, the unholy rule of my father seemed to control the night. His unannounced coming sliced the silence with terror. By his power, he stole freedom and killed imagination. Neither he nor the little three-year-old child knew that my spirit escaped each time, escaped with fragments of hope into the realm of the Holy.

When words first came they were confined to the day. Then it was safe to speak only of ordinary things. Wordless silence continued on in the night, where daytime language was forbidden, and the threat of hope was not allowed.

O Creator of the Universe, how could you endure, how could I endure, the breaking of my being into separate worlds? Yet what choice did I have? If I had stayed only in my father's world, hope itself would have been destroyed. I would not, nor could not, have known your love. I chose to break apart, to abandon myself to him, that my spirit could be with you and know your comfort and your love. The physician and the priest, they took my body. Into your hands my spirit flew.

◇◇◇◇◇

Was I awake or asleep, was I ready or not, when you, O Holy One, came in power and glory to judge me and claim me for yourself?

You came, heavily disguised in the garb of a friend, who was already your true priest and very different from those who had abused me. My friend-priest had few words to say. Even those he had, he left behind when he followed me into the terror and the madness of the night. Quietly, he witnessed the thunder of my rage. Silently, he held me while I screamed. Firmly, he accompanied me as I took my first steps from unknowing to knowing, from the unholy to the holy. He kept my body and soul together for me when I had no strength to do so for myself. His presence, like that of all good friends, gave me a glimpse of who I truly was. His presence, like that of all good priests, brought you, the Holy, into our midst.

You also came dressed as my physician, and wielded your power through the language she spoke. You took her gentle and reassuring speech and used it as your sword. Through the words she offered to me as a gift, you shredded the veil that had been my protection. You made me see the horrible truths that had broken my being into pieces: death-threats, torture, rape of my body as an infant, a little girl, and a young woman. In the glare of your shining light I saw the words and drugs, the ropes and knives, which my father wielded to trick, abuse, and control my body and mind. You led me to know what had never been forgotten: the brutality of men towards me and my siblings.

My physician continued to speak, refusing to be silenced by the horrors that answered. She is not to blame for what she unleashed; she only ever sought to heal. But I ask you, Holy One, was there no other way? When you came, could you not have judged my abusers for what they did, without having to judge me, their mere victim?

◇◇◇◇◇

Both friend and physician worked to restore me to myself. Through them you came unexpected. You entered my night and shattered all illusion. You gave me the courage to face what had happened, and thereby weakened the power of evil and overthrew those who had always controlled me. Then you waited for me. You waited to know whether I would resist or welcome your radical transformation of the only way I had known – the way of secrecy and lies, evil and submission.

I saw myself the battlefield where you, the Almighty, fought the cause of my terror and brokenness. I saw two different ways ahead. I could be like the soft earth that absorbs the soldiers' blood and grows green in the springtime. Or I could remain frozen in imagination and in time, dead to the possibility of new life, and unwilling to bear witness to your greater power and glory. I saw the way of life and blessing, and the way of alienation and death. I heard anew your command in the presence of my friend-priest and in the gift of my physician: "This day, choose life." I followed the example of my own spirit when a child, and promised to abide with the Holy forever.

Now I have language to help me speak and power with which to act. My mind and body are my own. Stolen innocence lends itself to courage, while broken trust is welded by love's strength. I have the freedom to join with others to name the evil of our time, to call for an end to the violation of creation, to confront the forces that permit wars to be waged, little children to starve, families to be terrorized, earth to be desecrated. I know the presence of the Holy in the very stuff of the world. Nothing can separate me from what is just and true. Everything invites me to keep my promise to live with the Holy forever. As I look backwards and forwards and turn again to what is now, I praise the Source of all that is.

Holy of holies,
the earth is yours and you are the earth.
The sky is yours and you are the sky.
The sea is yours and you are the sea.
The sun is yours and you are the sun.
Earth, sky, sea, and sun,
Holy One mine,
how dear you are.

Questions to ask ourselves

- What degree of predictable unpredictability was there in my childhood?
- What did I do to hang on to some power as a child?
- Who have I told about the suffering in my childhood?
- Who are the significant people in my life who have helped me know myself better?
- Who has helped me to know and trust God?
- Have I ever resisted going for counseling because of reluctance to confront some truths about my life?
- To what extent do I choose life and blessing over alienation and death in the small and not-so-small decisions about how to live today?
- How do I praise God?

Honoring truth

Honor your father and your mother, so that your days may be long in the
land that the Lord your God is giving you.

EXODUS 20:12

Of all the ten commandments given through Moses to the people, the one that children hear most often from their elders is the fifth, the one that speaks about honoring parents. In church and in Sunday school it is used to reinforce the notion that children must believe and behave as though their parents (and by extension all adults) are always right in everything they do.

This interpretation of the fifth commandment contrasts with the parable of the wooden bowls, from the Jewish tradition, which offers a different perspective.

Three generations of a family live together in one household. Every evening six people gather for supper: two elderly grandparents, their daughter and her husband, and a young boy and girl. In recent years, the grandparents have become increasingly frail and doddery. Their eyesight has deteriorated, and their coordination is not what it used to be. At mealtimes they can no longer eat without spilling some food on the table and on themselves, and sometimes one of them will accidentally knock their beautiful pottery dish to the floor where it shatters into a thousand pieces.

The younger generation – the old couple's daughter and her husband – come up with a series of solutions to this problem. So that they and their young children no longer have to eat supper at a messy table, first they bring in a second table just for the grandparents. Then, to prevent any more broken dishes, they get some cheap wooden bowls for the grandparents to use instead of pottery ones. (Wooden bowls in those days were equivalent to plastic bowls today.)

After this new supper arrangement has been in place for a few months, the young boy and girl busy themselves one day with some wood and carving tools. Their mother, curious, wonders what they are doing. They tell her:

"Mother, we are making two wooden bowls, one for you and one for father. They are for you when you grow old and can no longer sit at table with us without making a mess and without dropping the pottery dishes on the floor where they will shatter."

◇◇◇◇◇

In the parable of the wooden bowls, there are two sets of parents, and two sets of children. When the frail and elderly are pushed aside and supper is no longer shared around the same table, the community of the family is essentially destroyed. In the context of the fifth commandment, it illustrates how the middle generation fails to honor the older mother and father. It is the adults, not the children, who have broken the commandment.

Historically, the commandments were always meant for adults and not for children. When Moses came down from Mount Sinai, he delivered the ten commandments to an audience of men and women, not youngsters. It seems that over the years the Church has co-opted the fifth commandment to coerce children into doing what grownups want. The Church's message is "Young children, if you don't honor your mother and father, you are disobeying God."

Another meaning can be found in the parable if we focus on the younger children. They are the ones who, in making some wooden bowls for future use, point out the mistake their parents have made in sitting the grandparents at a different table. Is it wrong for children to let parents see the error of their ways? Is that honoring or dishonoring? Do the children break the fifth commandment?

The parable can be helpful for women and men whose parents abused or neglected them when they were young. Perhaps, at different stages in our healing, we will relate to different explanations. Anything which frees us to think through the oppressive and silencing influence of being told to honor our parents – or else – is a good thing. What does our Creator want, expect, or even demand, when parents themselves do not act or speak honorably? Does a young child who has been hurt by her/his parents and who subsequently speaks out about it, fail to honor them? Do abused children break the fifth commandment if they dare think that an abusive parent has wronged them? Do they invoke the wrath of an Almighty Power by telling the truth?

◇◇◇◇◇

During therapy, I have had to deal with my feelings towards my abusive father and my colluding mother many times. Each time I would make some progress. My strong, negative feelings would subside for a while, but eventually I would spiral around at a deeper level to still-unresolved feelings. If I pushed the feelings aside, they would manifest themselves as nightmares or anxiety attacks. I have learnt over the years to pay attention to what is going on inside, and to share it with someone – a friend or counselor – if I am not able to sort things out by myself.

The last time I brought up in counseling my poor relationship with my mother, my counselor said, "What you are struggling with is the commandment, 'Honor your father and your mother'." I was jolted by her comment. I wanted sympathy. I wanted her to listen to me rehearse one more time my catalogue of neglect and betrayal. I did not want to face having broken a scriptural commandment. Neither did I want to face the deep-seated guilt I had locked away. And I especially did not want to bring my faith to bear on the issue.

But, I have also learned over the years to trust that my counselor knows how and when to push me. Shortly after that particular session I wrote a meditation based on the fifth commandment, informed by the parable of the wooden bowls and by the book *Thou Shalt Not Be Aware*, in which the author Alice Miller equates the taboo of talking about childhood sexual abuse with an unspoken commandment not to remember abuse when it happens.

◇◇◇◇◇

O Creator, how long until I can come and stand before you with my head held high? I have been tormented for too long by the chaos in the depths of my being. I crouch down, shoulders hunched, hiding my face, lest anyone see the enormity of my guilt, or hear the anguish of my cries.

Honor your father and your mother, they told me, and without any further instruction they expected me to conform. It was like being an alien in a foreign land, forced to learn its language to survive. Honor your father and your mother. Tell everyone how good they are. Make them proud. Don't trespass on their territory. Don't question them, but pay attention to their every word. Be quick to obey and slow to complain.

Gradually, I learnt the customs and language of the country of my childhood. But I remained a foreigner, never fully belonging, always yearning for a different home.

As the years went by, the weight of the commandment bent me low. With my face always to the ground, the view before me was foreshortened. I only ever knew the immediate space and time of my existence. I was jealous of other children who stood so much taller than I, their faces lifted to the sky, their horizon miles away. Their vista held so many promises, as it beckoned them into unexplored territory and invited them to dream dreams of adventure, risk, and love.

Honor your father and your mother. Be obedient, keep out of their way, set all your complaints aside... I became so fluent in all of that, it was as though I fully belonged in that land. But how could I boast about their goodness when what they did was so bad as to betray their own honor? The only choice I had was to lie, especially since I was so young and had hardly begun to speak the language of truth that you, my Creator, intended me to learn. Single words were all I ever said, and then I murmured those quietly to myself in case someone heard me and accused me of breaking that unbreakable command. "Silence. Freedom. Alone. Elsewhere. Cry. Wait. Night." This was the vocabulary I tucked safely away in an inside pocket of my being.

Necessity taught me the only way to do everything that was expected of me was not to know the truth. "Honor your father and your mother" was actually code for "Do not be aware." I locked out the terrible truth from my consciousness, every facet of it imprisoned in its own cell. Betrayal, rage, knowledge, terror. If a cell became too full to accommodate any more of its particular truth I made another to house more recent arrivals. When the contents of one cell threatened to leak out through the bars and enter the neighboring cell, I built an isolation block. In this way, betrayal would never know that rage shared the same prison. Knowledge of the truth never communicated with the terror the truth bore. Then for the sake of complete security I appointed prison guards to keep watch over the inmates.

I alone was free. Free of responsibility for any part of the truth. Free not to lie. Free to honor my mother and my father. Free to live long in the land you, my Creator, had given.

Or so I thought. But this land where I lived was not my true home. There was a hollow place inside me, never satisfied, where my cries echoed endlessly. Almost too late I woke up one day and realized I had to leave my parents' homeland if I was ever to find peace. Could I leave and still honor them? Of course, I told myself, because once I had found how to fill the emptiness inside I intended to return.

I woke up and left home, not knowing where I was going except that the formless void within was calling me to dive down into its depths. I followed its voice, deeper and deeper into the waters of chaos, further and further away from the certainty of dry land. All the time I followed I became more and more awake. Through all the depths I traveled, I became more and more aware. Eventually when I had gone far enough, you, my Creator, met me in the chaos. You gave me enough strength to know the truth. My first glimpse was enough to know that I could never return to that place of not-knowing.

After I discovered my carefully constructed prison, I had to meet the prison guards and learn their names: Denial, Loyalty, Ambition, Pretense.

Having met the prison guards, I had to meet the prisoners. One by one I heard their stories: rape, torture, humiliation, death-threats, drugs. One by one I experienced for the first time the powerful emotions that had been locked up for so many years: fury, despair, grief, friendlessness. I also had to let them meet each other and take time to know each other. Together we all had to learn to respect and value one another.

O Holy Source of Life, you called me towards home, where I can know the truth and be set free. Yet the nearer I approached the home you promised the more distant it became. The land you held in trust, waiting for my arrival, has its own dangers. I need to build another prison in which to conceal my childhood of lies. Unless I forget the time before now, I am in grave danger of not honoring my father and my mother, and therefore of losing the land you give.

Holy Preserver of Truth, how can I remain silent about the abuse inflicted on me day and night? Knowing truth, how can I not tell truth? Telling truth, how can I not dishonor my parents, break your commandment, and lose all?

I know my offense. It is another chaos, threatening me even more than the first. For I have seen and tasted the gifts of your holy realm and can't bear to lose them. I hide my face from you in a vain effort to conceal my guilt. But like a homeless beggar with nothing left to lose I also plead with you not to hide your face from me.

Holy One, break me open to receive your grace. Lift up my eyes to see another way.

It is true, I did return to my parents' home, where I did a brave and foolish thing. In the spirit of love, I spoke the truth. I brought before my mother and my father the terrible things they had done to me and for just a moment recognition crossed over their faces. But then, very hurriedly, they put on their masks to conceal who they really are; I never saw them again. They said they were so sorry, but I must have lost my mind. They became angry when I did not relent. They disowned me as a daughter, and treated me like an outsider. They rallied their friends who joined in the chorus: "She's mad, she's a liar, she has forgotten the commandment. She's mad, she's a liar, she refuses to show honor. She's mad, she's a liar, she does not belong to us."

Mad? Perhaps. A liar? Yes, but in the past, not anymore. Forgotten the commandment? No; though I certainly knew I could not keep it anymore.

Holy One, break me open to receive your grace. Lift me up to see another way.

In the night you show me a vision of how you intended my parents to be. I see them without their masks. I see them shining, made in your image. I see them before they hurt me and used me. You show me that I was right to set before them the wrong that they did. You show me that I have honored them in holding before them the suffering they caused, for they too need to live with truth, not lies. I have honored them in reaching out to remove the masks from their faces. I have kept your commandment; I have been faithful to you.

In the night, when the vision recedes, a huge weight lifts from my shoulders. The guilt that never belonged to me is gone. I can breathe freely for the first time. As the shock of fresh air enters unused spaces of my lungs, your Spirit reaches into closed off crevices of my soul. I gasp in fright over the new thing you are doing.

In the night you have been waiting to take me home. Now I am ready. You help me to my feet. You take my face in your hands and lift it to your own. Through tears of joy, I see you twinkling with the stars in the night sky. Through surrender to your goodness, I know another way, your only way, which is the way of love.

Surely you do indeed break me open, and into my emptiness floods your grace.

◇◇◇◇◇

Questions to ask ourselves

- Is it liberating to realize the commandment to honor one's parents is meant more for adults than for young children?
- To what extent has honoring my parents been more important than honoring truth?
- What does the Creator want me to do about parents who have acted dishonorably?
- Do I feel guilty when I tell the truth about adults who hurt children?
- Can I cope with the rejection from family and friends who would prefer me not to tell the truth about childhood sexual abuse?
- What is my sense of "coming home" when I have confronted, or think about confronting, people who abused me in childhood?

Preparing for angels

"Then Jesus was led up by the Spirit into the wilderness to be tempted by the devil."

MATTHEW 4:1

The temptation of Jesus in the wilderness is traditionally read at the beginning of Lent, that season of the Church year when we focus on the suffering and death that preceded Jesus' resurrection. Sometimes we give something up during Lent to help us keep this focus. We give up sugar in our coffee, or maybe coffee itself. We give up sex or swearing, alcohol or meat. We usually manage to suffer a little. More importantly, we are tempted a lot. We begin to crave the very thing we have promised not to indulge in, as though our life depended on it. If we keep our commitment for the entire 40 days, we can learn some more about the nature of discipleship. We can learn some more about on what – and on whom – our life really depends.

The only other references to temptation in Matthew's gospel appear in the prayer that Jesus taught his disciples, "Lead us not into temptation," and in Jesus' instructions to his disciples in Gethsemane, "Stay awake and pray that you may not come into temptation." Given Jesus' own experience of being tempted in the wilderness immediately after his baptism and before he embarked on his ministry, why does he urge his disciples to pray to be kept from temptation? What is so terrible about it that he does not want them to endure? Or does Jesus have doubts about whether they could endure without giving in?

The setting of Jesus' time of temptation is the wilderness – barren, desolate, empty. Except if it was a sandy desert place, it would also be full of tiny gritty particles getting into every orifice, into eyes and ears, nostrils and hair, irritating mucous membranes and aggravating any cuts or scratches. Such a wilderness is worse than empty.

Such a place is not easily ignored. Yet the Spirit led him there.

◇◇◇◇◇

Jesus who was in the wilderness for 40 days and 40 nights understands what it is like for those of us who live in the wilderness associated with re-membering childhood trauma. Like desert sand blown up into thick clouds, our memories block everything else from our vision. There are so many re-minders around us. Sights and sounds that used to be ordinary and everyday become triggers that take us back ten, 20, 30 years or more. A young child playing alone in the park scrapes painfully at scars of raw vulnerability. A ball of twine in a hardware shop invokes memories of torture. The shrill sound of women's laughter transports us back to times of humiliation. The smell of fish in a tuna sandwich is a man's genitalia in our face when we were an infant.

There is nowhere to go where the memories are not. There is no escape from the craving for affection, safety, and peace. We are only here because the Spirit has led us here. We chose to follow because – in spite of everything – we cling to the promise of abundant life.

◇◇◇◇◇

He fasted 40 days and 40 nights, and afterwards he was famished. The tempter came to Jesus and said to him, "If you are the Son of God, command these stones to become bread." But he answered, "It is written, 'One does not live by bread alone, but by every word that comes from the mouth of God'."

MATTHEW 4:2-4

If Jesus really is the Son of God, he can get what he needs for himself by simply telling the stones to turn into bread. In this first temptation he sees an immediate solution to his physical hunger. If he had given in, he might have alleviated his short-term need, yet his resistance and his actual response suggest very strongly that his relationship with the Holy One would have been jeopardized. Jesus does not need to do some magic to prove to himself who he is. On the contrary, he needs to refrain from doing any magic, for only then will he remain dependent on all that the Creator has to give. Only then will he be in touch with the reality of all his needs and the richness of the Source of Life.

We too long for a quick fix to the agony we face when we first remember being abused. We are tempted to minimize the damage, rush through the healing process, and get on with our lives as though nothing had changed. We want to grab hold of anything that promises us a way out. If only we could convince ourselves that it did not really happen, then there would be no need for any more fuss. If only we knew exactly what he did, then that knowledge would suffice. If only we knew why she chose to hurt us, then understanding would diminish our pain. If only we could be sure what age we were when they stopped involving us in their secrets, we could stop having to deal with it now. Or we might imagine that if our adult lives were better we would not even have to revisit our childhood. If only I had a better job I would be fine. If only I owned my own home, finished my degree, could afford a new car, could have a month's holiday in the sun. If only... If only...

A similar temptation is to think that if we had been slightly different as children then we would never have been hurt. If only we had been better behaved. If only we had had good grades in school. If only we had found someone to tell. If only we had run away. If only we had been a boy, or a girl, or younger, or older, or prettier, or less attractive. If only we had not been ourselves. If only...

Our quick route of escape involves dumping blame for the horrible things that happened where it least belongs – on ourselves as children, and on ourselves as adults. The relief this brings from our desolation is at best brief, and at worst compounds and confuses our experience. To engage in the painstaking task of slowly unraveling the knot of childhood sexual abuse and identifying the many strands of rage, grief, terror and isolation, we have to resist anyone and anything that pretends to offer a quick and easy remedy. Of course we are tempted to believe that there is such a remedy. It's what any human being would want – yes, even Jesus. Having lived with the secret of sexual abuse, we have also learned to make do with a few scraps of all that we really need. We are too ready to settle for less than the fullness of life.

So although it will probably help to know more about the what, when, and why of the abuse, and although we do need food, shelter, warmth and human friendship, we need something more. Like Jesus, we also need a relationship with the Holy One, the One who creates us anew, sustains us in the struggle towards wholeness, and redeems the brokenness of our lives. Difficult though it may be, we have to exercise self-control, and not just gobble up the first remedy offered to us. Through faithful listening to the Spirit we will discern our deepest needs and be guided along the way to peace.

◇◇◇◇◇

> Then the devil took him to the holy city and placed him on the pinnacle of the temple, saying to him, "If you are the Son of God, throw yourself down; for it is written, 'He will command his angels concerning you,' and 'On their hands they will bear you up, so that you will not dash your foot against a stone'." Jesus said to him, "Again it is written, 'Do not put the Lord your God to the test'."
>
> MATTHEW 4:5-7

If Jesus really is the Son of God, he will always be loved by the Creator. If there is any doubt in Jesus' mind about this, the tempter has a solution. By jumping from the highest point of the temple, Jesus can test God's love and set his doubts aside permanently. Surely angels would act as a parachute and keep him safe. Why not let them take over responsibility for his well-being? What harm can come of it?

Yet again Jesus resists temptation, choosing instead to obey the commandment not to test God. Being in the wilderness does not reduce Jesus to a helpless victim. He refuses to manipulate the Creator into unusual displays of power. Instead Jesus holds on to his own power and continues to be responsible for himself.

Jesus' resistance to temptation is a challenging model to us as we wrestle with the demons in our own post-trauma wilderness. The balance of doubt and faith in our minds often tips towards doubt, and we long to be proved wrong. We long to bring on a show of extraordinary divine power that will resolve once and for all whether we are truly loved by the Holy. After all, if we are, then why did we have to suffer when we were young? Why do we suffer now? Our helplessness to prevent our abuse as children spills over into our life as adults, and threatens to keep us stuck in the role of helpless victim. We want to be rescued. We want to enlist the Creator's help in a scheme that will distract us from our doubts and our pain and land us safely on the other side of the healing work we have yet to do.

An extreme form is the temptation to suicide, a temptation many of us face at different times in our wilderness. We can rationalize it by telling ourselves that our Creator loves us no matter what we do, so even if we end our own life we will not risk losing that love. And what better escape from the misery and hard work of living with and healing from child sexual abuse? I cannot condemn those who contemplate – or attempt or actually commit – suicide. Neither can I agree with those who call suicide a long-term solution to a short-term problem, for I believe that love must seek to heal us even after death. Rather than being an escape or a solution, suicide only translates the process of healing to a different realm. But although suicide is an option, it is not the best one – and never the only one. Nothing is solved by testing our Creator's love.

We resist that temptation by clinging fast to our faith in the living presence of the Holy One, here with us now. We resist the temptation to manipulate anybody – human or divine – into rescuing us, by accepting responsibility for our actions, and – yes – also for our feelings and our memories. We might not like the feelings and memories we have, but they belong to us, and they have something to tell us. We have to befriend them, listen to them, learn from them, and accept them. We do not have to be victimized by them or rescued from them.

◇◇◇◇◇

Again, the devil took him to a very high mountain and showed him all the king-doms of the world and their splendor; and he said to Jesus, "All these I will give you, if you will fall down and worship me." Jesus said to him, "Away with you, Satan! for it is written, 'Worship the Lord your God, and serve only him'."

MATTHEW 4:8-10

The tempter is getting desperate to win Jesus away from God. There is nothing subtle about this temptation. He blatantly bribes Jesus with the promise of enormous wealth and power if only Jesus will worship him. And there is nothing subtle about Jesus' response either. He tells the tempter to get lost.

When we are at our weakest, we are very susceptible to the temptation to seize power that is not rightly ours. When we feel out of control – as we always do during unsought inundations of memories, flashbacks, nightmares, and disillusion – we thrash around looking for something to counter our helplessness. We might lash out at those closest to us, wanting to control them. We might plot revenge on the people who hurt us when we were small. We might distance ourselves from the very people who love us and can help us most, because we are not willing to risk any more.

Jesus insists that this is not the right way. Instead of grabbing power that will set us apart or place us over others, we have to stay open and vulnerable to others. Although our ability to trust has been eroded by the brokenness of our childhood, we have to muster whatever remnants we can and offer them to our Creator. Then we can expect love to reveal itself to us – but not on our terms, and not under our control. It's just as well really, since we would almost certainly get it wrong. Our imaginations are too small to encompass the vastness of love. Our experience is too limited to understand its mystery. Better to leave it to the Holy One, whom we see not in power and might, but in Jesus' willingness to hold on to truth, to look evil in the eye, and to say, "No."

◇◇◇◇◇

Then the devil left him, and suddenly angels came and waited on him.

MATTHEW 4:11

And so it is with us. When we resist the temptations to minimize our needs, or to play the role of victim, or to sacrifice truth for the sake of control, we loosen the hold of all the enemies who would impede our healing. We will be free for angels – in whatever form they choose to take – to care for us, nourish us, and accompany us on our way.

◇◇◇◇◇

Holy Creator, I cannot go where you are not.
Even in the wilderness you are with me,
    guiding, teaching, listening, being.
Yet I am so afraid:
    afraid that I will not be able to endure the hard road ahead;
    afraid that I will not even make it through tonight.
I am afraid of needing too much;
    afraid of feeling, knowing, hurting too much.
Holy One, I pray, take not your Spirit from me.

Like sap rising in a tree in the springtime
    I know your presence deep within,
    rising and filling every cell of my body,
    making my whole being upright and firm.
Sometimes I feel so strong;
    I wish it could always be that way.

But this I can do:
>I can return to you again and again,
>draw strength from you,
>and claim my own power,
>which by your grace is more than any magic,
>and, together with your love, is always sufficient.

In the wilderness there is no path,
>no way already trodden for me to follow.
I could go any way I choose.
I could go the way of revenge,
>or cynicism, or hatred, or despair.
I could go the way of self-pity, or self-loathing.
I could go the way of evil and lies.
Holy Creator, tonight I choose to go the way of my brother Jesus.
I will hold fast to truth.
I will open my hands, my heart, my soul,
>ready to receive anything or nothing.
I will wait for your peace to bring me home.

◇◇◇◇◇

Questions to ask ourselves

- Is there something in my life that I think I must have in order to cope? What would happen if I chose to give it up?
- What are the triggers of painful memories for me?
- How would I complete the sentence: "If only... then everything would have been (or would be) all right."
- Today, what do I need to take the next step towards wholeness?
- How do I take care of myself when confronted with difficult or frightening temptations?
- When do I distance myself from God?
- When am I most open to God?
- When have I experienced holy caring and accompaniment on my faith journey?

In solidarity with the Divine

And just as Moses lifted up the serpent in the wilderness, so must the Son of Man be lifted up, that whoever believes in him may have eternal life. For God so loved the world that he gave his only Son, so that everyone who believes in him may not perish but have eternal life. Indeed, God did not send the Son into the world to condemn the world, but in order that the world might be saved through him.

JOHN 3:14-17

For those of us seeking healing from sexual abuse in our childhood, the image of Jesus tortured on a cross is not necessarily helpful, in spite of the traditional teaching that the cross is somehow connected to our salvation. Indeed that teaching sometimes adds to our problems with the cross. However, as the central symbol of Christianity, the image continues to be before us in the Church's worship, prayers, hymns, theology, and sanctuaries. Is there any way that Jesus' suffering and death can speak to our struggles and pain in our quest for wholeness?

One strand of the tradition describes Jesus lifted up on the cross as atonement, that is, making up for something wrong with or missing from the world. Of course there is lots wrong with the world, and lots missing from it. It would be nice to have something to cancel out all the sins, and even Sin itself, but an increasing number of Christians admit they have trouble with this explanation of Jesus' death. It is very difficult to understand how a sacrifice 20 centuries ago helps little children who are being abused today. How does Jesus' execution make up for the love and caring that is missing from their lives? How does the cross save them?

We talk about the cross almost glibly, forgetting that it is an instrument of torture and execution. We gloss over the ruthless reality behind it. We prefer not to look too closely at the holy man Jesus, stripped naked and nailed by his hands and feet to the heavy wooden structure, and then lifted up in front of a crowd of curious onlookers. We turn away from his searing physical pain, made worse by the sun's heat; the loss of control of his bowels; the slow suffocation as the weight of his body compressed his chest and made breathing next to impossible. Not to mention his sense of betrayal, loss, grief, failure, humiliation, and abandonment.

If all of this was so that evil could triumph for just three short days, and was definitively overcome by the greater power of goodness as seen in the Resurrection, maybe it was worthwhile. Maybe there is a holy logic to it. But any reasonable person can see that evil is still alive and well in our world. Even – or especially – a little child knows that.

Or what if the cross was Jesus taking on all the sins of the world and being punished instead of us? That's an alternate explanation. Maybe that works for people who've never been "punished" themselves, but for those of us who as children were told we deserved to be abused, or who made sense of our suffering by assuming we must have done something very bad, it doesn't.

Imagine: a six-year-old child is brainwashed into believing that Jesus died for her sins. That's how bad she is. That's how much power her badness has – it can kill the very best person that ever lived.

Then imagine: another six-year-old child is also brainwashed into believing that Jesus died for her sins. She also feels she must be very bad, only she feels even worse than this because at night Grandpa comes into her bed and touches her and makes her feel terrible all over. Before he goes he says, "Now you be a good girl and don't say anything about this to anyone, you hear me? And if you're very good, maybe Grandpa won't have to do this to you anymore." The power of this little girl's badness not only killed the very best person that ever lived, it also made Grandpa do horrible things to her. Her only hope is to do what he says – be very good and not tell anyone. Then at least she will save him from the shame of people knowing what he did. She will save herself from the shame of people knowing how bad she is – so bad that even Jesus "dying for her sins" wasn't enough punishment.

If this is what the cross is all about, then we ought to tear down every one of them from the church steeples, rip them off the walls, and clear them from the altars. We ought to smash them, burn them, melt them down, destroy them, and with them the outdated theology that says God is all-powerful and humanity is all-sinful. If the Son of God has to go too, then so be it.

◇◇◇◇◇

But what if we simply see in Jesus' crucifixion a sign that he knew about suffering because he experienced it first-hand? It doesn't matter if he was human or divine, or both, his suffering was real; we can relate to him on that level, and he to us. If Jesus is divine then we are connected to the Divine in our suffering. If Jesus is human then we can learn from his connection to the Divine and appropriate it for ourselves. Either way, we are assured that the Holy One cares passionately about us in our pain and anguish.

We must, however, acknowledge an important difference between Jesus' suffering and that of an innocent child. Jesus suffered because of his freely chosen stand against oppression; children who are sexually abused suffer simply because of their vulnerability. There is no element of choice in it for them. Only later, as adults, do we have a choice about facing the suffering we endured and claiming wholeness and life for ourselves. In Jesus' willingness to risk his personal safety for the sake of compassion and justice, he provides us with inspiration and a challenging role model.

◇◇◇◇◇

Jesus, when I look at the cross,
    I see you hanging,
        utterly helpless, utterly vulnerable, utterly alone.
As I look, I weep.
As I weep, I remember.
Hanging there, poised on the brink of death,
    you invite me to return and reclaim my own self.

You don't make me do this, but in truth I know this:

> that if I want to stay with you I have to be here with all of who I am.

> I have to be here with the ugliness of the past that I so often deny.

> I have to be here with the struggle of the present that I would rather avoid.

> I have to be here with the promise of the future that I hardly dare believe.

Jesus, I am afraid.

I am afraid of you, your weakness, your pain.

I am afraid when you cry out in agony, because there is nothing I can do.

I am afraid of your eyes pleading with me, not because you hold me responsible,

> but because I can neither bear nor relieve the injustice of what is going on.

I am afraid, because when I see you I also see my sister,

> naked, face down on the table,

> arms outstretched, tied by her wrists,

> being raped by the priest.

I am afraid because just as no one helped you, no one helped her.

I am afraid, because so are you, and you want us – you need us – to be with you.

Jesus, I am angry.

I am angry with myself for being powerless to help.

I am angry with the forces of evil that nailed you to the cross.

I am angry with all evil forces that cause unjust suffering and death.

I am angry with the Church that teaches God is all-powerful.

Surely, if that was so, you would not be hanging on the cross.

I am angry with my sister for being so vulnerable, and for turning to me for help.

I am angry with you for being such a hard role model to follow.

Jesus, I am proud.

I am proud of you for standing up for truth.

I am proud of your persistence, your faithfulness, your love.

I am proud of the women, amongst them your mother, who watched you die.

I am proud of the Church for claiming your story as its own.

I am proud of my sister for not being passive, for struggling to get free.

I am proud of myself for finding my way here and daring to stay.

Jesus, I am sad.

When I see you hanging, I know my own loss,

    yet I can only imagine yours:

    your loss of friendship, mission, and hope,

    the death of your body, and your surrender to the Holy One.

For myself, I grieve the loss of childhood before it hardly began.

I grieve the death of innocence and trust.

I grieve the death of true family, of sisterhood,

    of laughter and love.

Hanging there, poised on the brink of death,

    you invite me to return and reclaim my own self.

I am filled with grief and anger, fear and pride.

I connect for the first time with parts of myself I had left strewn about

    and treated like old rubbish of no value to me.

Because of you, I am gathered up into one with all who I am.

Because of you, my past is carried forward and brought into now.

Because of you, I have a new starting place for whatever lies ahead.

◇◇◇◇◇

Questions to ask ourselves

- What have I been taught at Sunday school or at church about the meaning of Jesus' death on the cross?
- What do I believe today about the cross?
- How does Jesus' suffering speak to my own – as a child? as an adult?
- Do my beliefs about Jesus' suffering alleviate my own suffering?
- What would I like to say to Jesus, or to the Divine, today? What do I imagine the response might be?

Part 2

Community

Invitation to community

At that time Jesus said, "I thank you, Father, Lord of heaven and earth, because you have hidden these things from the wise and the intelligent and have revealed them to infants; yes, Father, for such was your gracious will. All things have been handed over to me by my Father; and no one knows the Son except the Father, and no one knows the Father except the Son and anyone to whom the Son chooses to reveal him.

"Come to me, all you that are weary and are carrying heavy burdens, and I will give you rest. Take my yoke upon you, and learn from me; for I am gentle and humble in heart, and you will find rest for your souls. For my yoke is easy, and my burden is light."

MATTHEW 11:25-30

One of the many reports of child sexual abuse that I have heard about concerns a little girl and her stepfather, a successful businessman. He used to come into the girl's bedroom at night, reach his hands under the bedclothes, and stroke her all over. She used to pretend to be asleep because the stroking made her feel weird. In a way she liked it, but mostly she wanted it to stop. Sometimes her stepfather would climb on top of her, and force his penis into her mouth. She hated it when he did that. It hurt so much, she could hardly breathe, and she couldn't make a sound. She would struggle to push him off, but he simply took her small arms in his huge hands and pinned her down to the mattress. She was powerless to get away from him.

What saved her was a picture that hung above her bed, a picture of Jesus with some sheep in a sunny meadow. When she could no longer bear the pain of what her stepfather was doing to her, she would remember the picture, and go to play with Jesus in the meadow. There she would feel calm and warm and cared for. The sheep were gentle, the flowers were very pretty, and Jesus was ever so kind. He let her stay there as long as she wanted; he never pushed her away, never told her to go home and back to bed.

Usually when people hear the phrase "child sexual abuse" they don't think about or imagine the complexity of the child's experience. Confusion, extreme physical pain, terror, and creative self-preservation are all present. The latter does not in any way reduce the degree of suffering. It is simply a way to endure. Vacating one's body to find a temporary refuge away from the violence is a dreadful choice to have to make. When the little girl escaped into the safety of the picture to be with Jesus, she was drawing on reserves of power that ought not need to be tapped; yet it was the only way she could make the unbearable less than the whole of her reality.

Matthew's gospel reports Jesus thanking the Creator for hiding "these things" from the wise and intelligent, but making those same things known to infants. Abusive adults are generally intelligent and often well educated. They might well be considered wise by the world's standards. Yet they have no clue about the impact of their actions, and no clue about the survival mechanisms of their victims. They have separated themselves from the Holy One, who in turn keeps hidden from them the miraculous abilities and power of the children they hurt. Little ones know how to find holiness in the midst of the unholy. The Holy One speaks, saying, "Come to me and I will give you rest," and reveals to those who need it most a safe retreat and a way to cope.

Even non-abusive adults sometimes show their ignorance about the reality of children's lives. Just a few years ago I heard a minister preaching on Matthew 11:28: "Come to me, all you that are weary and are carrying heavy burdens, and I will give you rest." He began his sermon by recalling the church he attended as a child, and in particular the Communion table on which was written the verse from Matthew 11. Then he went on to say, "Of course, as children none of us could possibly understand what those words meant. We were all so carefree and unburdened in our youth."

This simplified and sentimental view of childhood is unhelpful both to children who experience abuse or other difficulties in life, and to adults who did not grow up in a happy and protected environment. The message that children are lucky because they have nothing to worry about is not only untrue; it also tells adults they don't need to listen to children or take them seriously. If children live in bliss, then anything they might say is unimportant to adults whose lives are so much more complex and potentially troubled.

Another danger in not acknowledging the painful aspect of some children's reality is the message given to adults struggling to heal from a painful childhood. The temptation to minimize what happened and to keep it locked up in the past is already very strong. It is hard enough for those of us abused as children to trust listeners who are sympathetic; it is most unlikely we will share our stories in a church setting when "helping professionals" publicly exhibit little understanding. Yet we need so much to be able to talk, and pray, and simply be, with our community of faith, with all of who we are, with all of the ugliness that was done to us, with all of the terrible, terrifying range of emotions with which we wrestle as we heal.

When we were young we found ways to cope, just like the little girl who went off to play with Jesus in the meadow. Now as adults we need something different. We need to be less alone in our struggle and in our suffering. We need a community that cares enough – even if it doesn't understand completely – to invite us in, to say to us: "Come, all you who work so hard to regain trust and self-respect; come, all you who are weighed down with rage and grief and shame; come to us, and we will give you a safe place where your tears are honored, where your story is believed, where you can set down the burden of your past, and where you can rest."

Jesus said, "Come to me…and I will give you rest." Any church that seeks to continue the work of Jesus must also say, "Come to this community of faith… and we will give you rest." This is what discipleship is about. This is what we mean when we say believe in incarnation. We believe in the Holy Spirit being embodied in our faith communities, speaking through us, doing the holy work of hospitality through our hands and feet, through our words of welcome and intentional listening.

In order to be hospitable the church has to work doubly hard. Over the last two decades many people have come forward and spoken out about being sexually abused by church leaders. Sometimes the abuse took place in churches or in buildings connected to the church. It is no wonder that on hearing the words "church" and "abuse" in the same sentence, we tend to think "abusive church." The church not only has to change this perception, it also has to find ways to extend a sincere invitation to people with painful experiences of abuse.

The church has long been able to reach out and care for members with physical illness, but has not done so well in tending to those with other wounds. Surely the time is ripe for the church to learn from the reflection of one woman, being treated for cancer. She spoke about the extensive support and caring available to help her, from understanding and knowledgeable medical staff, to provisions for child care when she had to go for radiation treatments, to casseroles from her church, to support groups for herself and her partner, to being included in the prayers of intercession in weekly worship. Then she added, "If only there had been the same kind of support when I was going through therapy to heal from having been sexually abused as a child…"

If only churches knew just how much work it takes to heal childhood pain, surely they would drive people to counseling appointments, look after their children, ensure they didn't have to be alone overnight, prepare meals, and provide opportunities for conversation and prayer. Thankfully, here and there, change is taking place.

One of the participants in a church Bible study group had to be hospitalized when she first began to deal with her abuse. Since she was unable to attend Bible study at the church, the priest arranged for the group to meet at the hospital instead. By using a little imagination, that church was able to be community for the woman in the midst of her suffering. Week by week she made ready a small room in the hospital for her friends to come and be church with her. She tidied away the cards and board games, put the magazines and books on the shelves, wiped down the table and placed on it a few flowers, a candle, and a Bible. In an extraordinary way, the most vulnerable member became the host to that particular incarnation of the church. The yoke of faith was revealed as blessing to all concerned.

In another church a minister was asked to officiate at the wedding of a couple who never attended church, but whose parents were church members. Conversation with the couple revealed that one of them was extremely anxious attending church, and especially about having the marriage ceremony in the church. Her uncle, a priest, had sexually abused her in one of his churches. The minister explored different options with the couple, including holding the ceremony elsewhere. Over the next few months the minister met with the couple together and separately, listening to their needs, hopes, and dreams. As trust developed, it became possible for the person whose uncle had abused her to enter the sanctuary and feel comfortable and even comforted in that space. A measure of healing had occurred. A laying down of burdens carried alone for a long time had taken place.

◇◇◇◇◇

During my own journey towards wholeness, I have been accompanied and strengthened by belonging to a faith community. I have experienced caring and support not only from individuals, but also from the community as a whole. I have found the most effective help within communities who are confident about who they are, and are willing to let me be who I am.

For a few years I worshipped often with the Religious Society of Friends, or Quakers. The following reflection is about the invitation to community that I found in their Meetings for Worship.

Here I am, Sunday morning,
> five minutes earlier than the posted time,
> and the door to the Meeting House is locked.

Am I too early or too late,
> or do I enter downstairs?

Downstairs: I can hear voices inside.

This door opens, I go in.

People smile and welcome me, and I am shy,
> dive into the washroom before ascending
> upstairs to a spacious room.

Yes, I say when asked, it is my first time.
> Thank you. I'll be fine, but
> how do I know? I don't.

Chances are, I won't.

Anything might happen in a whole hour of silence.

I remember two things from that Meeting.

First, the Call to Worship,
> which no one spoke,
> no one read or sang or danced or expressed outwardly
> in any form whatsoever,
> but it was the loudest call I had ever heard
> in over thirty years of Anglican and United attendance.

This call was issued as one by one we worshippers entered
> quietly finding a place to sit
> then sat, expectantly
> waiting,
>> waiting for what?

So much anticipation of the Holy One
    coming to be amongst us,
    it would have been rude for her to stay away.
It would have been rude for any one of us
    to be less than fully present
    to the deep and deepening silence
    that collected us into one holy chorus
    of wordless, soundless, thunderous praise.

The second thing I remember from that Meeting
    is recalling without wanting to
    the enforced silence of nighttime horror
    when to make a sound was the greatest folly,
    to formulate words was beyond my childhood power,
    and to let memory seep into the following day
    was an act of supreme madness.
Then my only option was to keep silence,
    even though into that unholy quiet
    the Holy came, gathered me up
    and carried me away for a while
    until the worst was over and it was possible to return.
Silence, then, was wise and cruel
    unholy and holy,
    made and kept in isolation from the world,
    witnessed honestly by no other human being.
This earlier silence I remembered
    as I sat in silence with others
    by choice, free choice.

How could this be,
    this seeking and being sought,
    this finding and being found,
    in company with women and men,
    all strangers to me?
How could this be,
    this only-wise-and-holy quiet time
    shared with thirty, forty people
    and no one getting hurt,
    or being threatened?
What miracle of grace was extended to me
    as we sat together speechless,
    spirit singing to spirit
    in a roomful of humanity
    desiring only Love!

Another time, another city, another Meeting,
    yet the same gracious invitation
    and grace-filled power beyond words
    contained within that sacred hour.
Some of these Friends were no longer strangers.
I had been here before and recognized many,
    yet in this sanctuary I hardly knew myself.
One by one we entered the room;
    together we entered the silence.
Surrounded by the safe company of Friends,
    I slipped beyond any place I had been before
    to the conjuncture of silence, pain and grief.

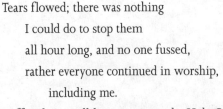

Tears flowed; there was nothing
    I could do to stop them
    all hour long, and no one fussed,
    rather everyone continued in worship,
        including me.
I offered my well-kept secrets to the Holy One,
    witnessed now by a faithful assembly
    whose simple presence honored my agony.

Later I would find a few words,
    inadequate to describe fully the reason for my tears
    and yet sufficient to show my trust
    and more than that, my gratitude,
    for their accompaniment of me
    backwards and forwards,
    reclaiming life.

Some of them in turn thanked me for my weeping,
    for through it, they said,
    I let them know the strength of being together,
    and the grace that goes with good listening in the Spirit.

◇◇◇◇◇

Questions to ask ourselves

- What early experiences of the Creator do I remember?
- When has a community of faith revealed the Holy One to me in such a way as to address my deepest needs?
- How has my worldly wisdom been a barrier between myself and my faith?
- Have I ever felt excluded from church community because of painful life experiences I thought my church would not want to know about?
- How often do I know a sincere and open invitation from my church to speak painful truth? What happens when I do?
- Can I be fully myself in my faith community, or must I leave some parts behind in order to "belong"?
- Are there other groups of people in my life who offer me relief from some of the weight of my past?

Good and necessary friends

"As the Father has loved me, so I have loved you; abide in my love. If you keep my commandments, you will abide in my love, just as I have kept my Father's commandments and abide in his love. I have said these things to you so that my joy may be in you, and that your joy may be complete.

"This is my commandment, that you love one another as I have loved you. No one has greater love than this, to lay down one's life for one's friends. You are my friends if you do what I command you. I do not call you servants any longer, because the servant does not know what the master is doing; but I have called you friends, because I have made known to you everything that I have heard from my Father. You did not choose me but I chose you. And I appointed you to go and bear fruit, fruit that will last, so that the Father will give you whatever you ask him in my name. I am giving you these commands so that you may love one another."

JOHN 15:9-17

Love one another. This is the simplest form of the new commandment that Jesus gives to his disciples, stated two chapters earlier in the gospel of John (13:36). Love one another. It is so simple and yet so hard for anyone to fulfill, regardless of the circumstances of our lives. For anyone who has known a deficit of love in their childhood, understanding the commandment presents particular challenges, as does working to fulfill the commandment. However, I strongly believe our capacity to "love one another" depends on far more than the measure of love we appeared to receive in our growing up years.

Jesus' elaboration sets out how to love one another, namely, "as I have loved you." He continues to say that people are his friends provided that they carry out his commands. Loving one another brings Jesus' followers into friendship with him and, through him, to the Creator. Loving one another is not only about human friendship; it also invokes a strong connection to the Holy.

Friendship for children who have suffered sexual abuse can be hazardous terrain to venture into, yet at the same time friendships outside of the abusive situation can be enormously beneficial. First, though, there is an absolute necessity for secrecy that must be taken care of. For if anyone finds out that the child has been or is being abused, all manner of terrible threats might come true.

There is the threat of punishment: "I will have to let Mommy (or God, or Santa Claus, or Jesus) know what a bad girl you are if you tell anyone"; "I'll take my belt to you"; "I won't be able to get you that nice new bike after all."

There is the threat of abandonment: "Your grandma and grandpa won't be able to look after you when your parents are away, and you'll be left all alone."

There is the threat of death: "If you tell, I'll kill myself" (or kill you, or your baby brother whom you love so much).

Another factor that must be overcome, or in some way compensated for, is isolation. Abusive families afraid of being discovered might impose severe restrictions on interactions with other children. Such restrictions can also be self-imposed by abused children who want to hide their shame, or who suppose that closeness with anyone will inevitably lead to getting hurt.

Shame, fear, isolation, and secrecy are realities to some degree for all sexually abused children. They hinder the development of friendships. By grace, there can also be other, more beneficial, realities – though these in no way justify or condone abuse. Some children seem to respond to pain in their own lives by being more sensitive and sympathetic to the needs and desires of others; such a disposition actually favors making close friends. Some children find distraction from their own pain by an intense and passionate interest (for example in sports, or drama, or music) which provides an avenue for friendship with others. Some abused children use their imagination to create relationships with pets or nature that would not ordinarily be called friendships, yet still call forth love and allow for holiness to be tasted.

Adults who are engaged in an intentional process of healing from childhood abuse do well to remember the friends they had as youngsters, for there is strength to be garnered from remembering goodness and love. Perhaps there was a close bond with a brother or sister; perhaps there was a school friend who accepted at face value restrictions such as never coming over to play when a certain family member was at home; maybe there was a special attachment to the family dog; maybe there was a particular place of retreat that allowed for safety and connection. Wherever there was an experience of loving one another, something holy was taking place. Being in touch with such childhood experiences helps us to overcome barriers of making and maintaining friendships as an adult; and it helps us to be aware of – and not overlook, or take for granted - the depth of meaning and love that already exists in some of our present relationships.

Jesus commands the disciples, "Love one another as I have loved you… You are my friends when you do what I command you." As a friend, Jesus emphasizes love over obedience, mutuality over inequality. Intimacy is more important than politeness; risk and vulnerability are more important than predictability. Yet if we were hurt as children we often prefer obedience because following rules is something we were trained to do. Inequality is easy for us when it perpetuates our early conditioning about ourselves. Intimacy can be a strange and frightening concept; we might well have structured our adult lives to be as risk-free as possible. So how do those of us who were hurt as children manage to be the kind of friend that Jesus was?

Our first forays into healing from sexual abuse involve disobedience to the rule of secrecy, which in itself is a huge risk. Talking about being abused is not a polite thing to do; rather, a degree of intimacy must first be established between speaker and listener. Although we might be committed to the healing journey, the outcome is far from certain. When we set off on such a journey, for ourselves or to accompany others, we inevitably practice loving one another. Though the journey is fraught with difficulties, and many obstacles will have to be overcome, having friends along the way ensures that the Holy One travels with us.

◇◇◇◇◇

"Love one another" says the Christ,
as though it were a command –
       like take out the garbage
       or pick up your clothes –
a simple thing I may or may not do.
       I am free to rebel or comply.

"Love one another, as I have loved you,
       laying down my life for you."
Christ, are you serious? Do you expect me
       to answer, "Yes of course,
       it's just what I've been waiting to do all my life"?
Were you absent after all, when at a tender age
       I lay down my body for the sadistic pleasure of others?
Did you not know that it cost me
       my dignity, my freedom, my life?

I have no more life to lose.
So with your permission, or without it –
       it's up to you –
I'll set about the business of reclamation.

My little sister and I used to share a room,
       and when necessary also a bed.
Huddled close together we intertwined our arms and legs
       in a serious endeavor to maximize the comfort we could afford one another
       without a word as to why we needed to do this.
We had our own innocent secrets that kept other secrets at bay.

A teenage friend from the other side of the tracks
        telephoned when forbidden to visit.
I knew without being told that her father was drunk again
        and therefore dangerous
        and we would chatter on and on about nothing in particular
        to ward off the dread that night would likely bring.

In springtime when the green was coming in
        I used to climb the chestnut tree out front.
Hidden high I loved my universe;
I followed insect travelers on their arduous ascent
        and on one occasion, for the sake of wonder, broke open three sticky buds
        to learn the pattern of their making.

All summer long I took refuge in my lofty place,
        lush leaves concealing my limbs,
        rough bark imprinting itself on my flesh
        lest I forget its necessary beauty.

By the time autumn blustered in
        I had learnt to stretch myself thin against the trunk
        imagining my body invisible as chestnuts inside their prickly case.
Green gave way to orange, red and brown,
        convincing me my universe loved me.

With winter came the stark reality
    of black branches that had framed my world a while.
I will never forget the beautiful necessity
    of a skeleton not my own,
    a lover with whom to trust my deepest desires.

The invitation to the city
    for three whole days of meeting with colleagues
    to address life on the margins and isolation in ministry
    was a welcome blessing.
And I wrote back,
Yes.

In no time at all
    strangers became fast friends.
We disclosed all manner of secret longings
    and disappointments and we made rash promises
    to keep in touch
    trusting Canada Post to be our liaison.

Only at the airport, waiting
    for our separate planes to come and fly us
    home where we didn't fully belong,
    did you tell me how he used to hurt you at night.
My mouth must have dropped;
    you could have been talking about my life.
How had we spent seventy-two hours together with
    not a word about what mattered most?

We sat on the airport floor side by side
    spilling secrets faster than we knew how
    yet knowing not to ask for more than what was offered:
        feeling each other's pain
        healing but not yet healed
        making up for lost time
        learning much from each other
        breaking the terrible isolation of our past
        risking our lives for the sake of love.

Your flight left first.
You were gone before me.
I never had a chance to say thank you
    – except to the One who sat with us –
    for turning my world upside down.

Today my little sister and I are both middle-aged.
We have helped each other heal
    through the love we have for one another.
Letters, phone calls, visits,
    breaking family traditions of secrecy and denial,
    sharing little victories,
    celebrating signs of triumph.
Yet remains the memory of watching the other
    tortured, and taken to the brink of death,
    too much to bear, both then and now,
    driving me to utter a prayer of invocation.
We can only love one another,
    because Another first loved us.

Befriending by the Holy that helped me speak
    pulls me deeper with the passing years
    into a new and beautiful silence,
        born of love alone.

◇◇◇◇◇

Questions to ask ourselves

- Where did I find friendship as a youngster?
- What happens when I say "Thank you" to the Holy One for friends?
- Am I polite and predictable with my friends rather than intimate? What are the obstacles that block me from taking risks?
- Who are the friends willing to walk with me on the difficult stretches of my journey towards wholeness?
- To what extent do I feel myself befriended by the Divine?

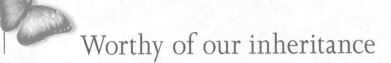

Worthy of our inheritance

"When the Son of Man comes in his glory, and all the angels with him, then he will sit on the throne of his glory. All the nations will be gathered before him, and he will separate people one from another as a shepherd separates the sheep from the goats, and he will put the sheep at his right hand and the goats at the left.

"Then the king will say to those at his right hand, 'Come, you that are blessed by my Father, inherit the kingdom prepared for you from the foundation of the world; for I was hungry and you gave me food, I was thirsty and you gave me something to drink, I was a stranger and you welcomed me, I was naked and you gave me clothing, I was sick and you took care of me, I was in prison and you visited me.'

"Then the righteous will answer him, 'Lord, when was it that we saw you hungry and gave you food, or thirsty and gave you something to drink? And when was it that we saw you a stranger and welcomed you, or naked and gave you clothing? And when was it that we saw you sick or in prison and visited you?'

"And the king will answer them, 'Truly I tell you, just as you did it to one of the least of these who are members of my family, you did it to me.' Then he will say to those at his left hand, 'You that are accursed, depart from me into the eternal fire prepared for the devil and his angels; for I was hungry and you gave me no food, I was thirsty and you gave me nothing to drink, I was a stranger and you did not welcome me, naked and you did not give me clothing, sick and in prison and you did not visit me.'

"Then they also will answer, 'Lord, when was it that we saw you hungry or thirsty or a stranger or naked or sick or in prison, and did not take care of you?' Then he will answer them, 'Truly I tell you, just as you did not do it to one of the least of these, you did not do it to me.' And these will go away into eternal punishment, but the righteous into eternal life."

MATTHEW 25:31-46

The passage is designated to be read on the last Sunday of the Church year, the Sunday that marks the Reign of Christ. Elements of warning, judgment, and surprise are all present in today's apocalyptic gospel text, just as they are in the gospel readings for the first Sunday of the year at the beginning of Advent. In this sense, moving through the year from Advent to the Reign of Christ takes more of a circular or spiraling process than a linear one.

The vision of a divine enthronement, in the company of heavenly angels and all earthly nations, sets out the basis for judgment that will take place when Christ comes in glory. Those who have cared for the hungry and the thirsty, the naked and the sick, the stranger and the imprisoned will be welcomed into eternal life; those who have failed to care will be banished into eternal punishment. There is nothing too surprising in that. What can be bewildering is Christ's clear identification with those in need. Christ says: "You fed me, you clothed me, you welcomed me," and people ask, "When did we do that?" "Whenever you did it to anyone in need, you did it to me," he answers. Christ our judge is the sick, the naked, the starving, the hungry, the thirsty, and the imprisoned here on earth. There is nothing in this text about our judge being an old white man with a long beard and flowing robes up in the sky.

There is nothing here that authorizes us to judge other people on the basis of age, gender, race, class, sexuality, or religious affiliation.

In any situation of child sexual abuse, three distinct parties are involved. Obviously there is the perpetrator who carries out the abuse, and the victim who is abused. But there is also the bystander, the person who is aware of the abuse taking place, either because he or she was present at the time, or, as is more often the case, by finding out about it afterwards.

Almost always children show signs when something wrong has happened, though there are many ways that they do this. They might have unusual bruising or unexplained bleeding. They might blurt out for no obvious reason, "I'm never going back there again," or "I hate him." They might be more explicit: "He put his hands down my pants." "Sometimes he comes into my bed at night." Other signs can include withdrawal, aggression, nightmares, or a sudden change in appetite.

Bystanders are shown these signs. They have a responsibility to recognize them and to follow through appropriately. Even long after the abuse has stopped, bystanders continue to play a role. Knowing that an adult friend or family member was abused as a child invites an open-minded, understanding, and proactive response.

It is in the spirit of the gospel to include amongst the people with whom Christ identifies, and by whom we are judged, the abused. As bystanders, we turn a blind eye and a deaf ear at our peril. Indeed, it is a matter of eternal life. In some respects the needs of the abused overlap with the needs of the stranger and the sick – they need to be welcomed and cared for. However, they have another unique need – to be believed. If as bystanders we do not believe what the abused tell us, then no real relationship is possible. If we do not take them seriously, we cannot receive their blessing.

Unfortunately, when children or adults reveal directly or indirectly that they have been abused, their disclosures are not always recognized, or welcomed. Often, bystanders do not want to know what happened. They are unwilling or unable to comprehend the impact of abuse. Their responses range from non-committal to shocking, from dismissive to defensive.

For example:

- A mother says to her adult daughter, "I was abused too. My abuse was worse than yours, so don't expect me to feel sorry for you."
- A brother to his sister: "There's no way Dad would ever do anything like that. You're making it all up."
- A priest to a congregational member, who has revealed being abused as a young boy by another priest: "I've listened to you, and I've talked to my colleague. He says he had nothing to do with abusing you when you were a child. I'm sorry, but there's nothing else I can do to help you."

- A mother to a young child: "It's not nice to say those ugly things about him when he looks after you every day after school. You know I have to work, so you should be glad he doesn't mind helping us out."

Thankfully, not all bystanders show this kind of indifference. Society's increased awareness of child sexual abuse and its seriousness means that many more people respond in helpful, proactive ways than ever before.

Some contemporary fiction reflects the shift from minimizing and denial to acknowledgement and intervention.

In the movie version of The Shipping News by Annie Proulx, Quoyle learns that his aunt Agnis was raped and made pregnant by her brother, Quoyle's father, when she was 12 years old. Agnis is now a middle-aged, down to earth woman, somewhat abrupt, but sensitive and with a fine sense of humor. She has been a part of Quoyle's life, keeping an eye out for him and his child, ever since Quoyle's wife was killed in a car accident. Following his cousin's revelation, Quoyle could perpetuate the decades-old silence, or he could take the opportunity to reciprocate her kindness. He remembers a comment Agnis made when a woman was reported to have cut off her abusive partner's head: "A good thing too. He must have deserved it." At the time her vehement reaction shocked Quoyle, but now – given what he knows about her terrible experience as an adolescent – he understands. He tells his aunt he knows about the rape and subsequent pregnancy by saying to her, "Some women should chop off their brother's head." His is not a neutral knowing of mere facts. He lets her know that he shares in her anger; that it is safe to trust him with her pain. "Have a cup of tea," he continues. "It'll keep you going." These words echo what Agnis had said to him in the early days of his grief after his wife died.

In No Time to Say Goodbye, by Sylvia Olsen, Vivian is an older student at a residential school for First Nations children. When she realizes that a younger girl Monica is in danger of being molested by the priest Father Maynard, she warns Monica to keep out of his way. Tearfully, Monica tells Vivian that Maynard has already molested her; Vivian is furious and promises to stop Maynard from hurting her anymore. First, Vivian tells Sister Mary Louise never to call Monica by the nickname Maynard uses for her. Then she goes to see Maynard in his office, and tells him that she knows he is abusing one of the girls, just as he had abused her, and that she is going to tell the police and everyone who comes to visit the school until he stops. Maynard starts to slap Vivian around, but the girl defends herself, and demands that Maynard leave. Within a few days the police have been told about the abuse at the school, and Maynard has left. With great courage, Monica stands up for Vivian when Sister Mary Louise says mean things about her.

Whenever bystanders actively bear witness to abusive situations that they see and hear and learn about, they move towards right relationship and receive blessing from the Holy One. However, as they speak out, they also risk invoking trouble, losing security, being stripped of power, and being denounced by other bystanders and by perpetrators of abuse.

Such witnesses can themselves be victimized. This is clearly seen in the case of two pediatricians, Drs. Higgs and Wyatt, while practicing at a hospital in the north of England in the late 1980s. Based on routine medical examination of children admitted to the hospital, they diagnosed many cases of suspected child sexual abuse (in other words, other causes having been considered and excluded, the most likely cause of their patients' problems was sexual abuse – therefore it needed to be considered and either excluded or confirmed). The doctors acted according to their legal responsibility, to notify the police and social service agencies who had the power – as the doctors did not – to investigate.

Children were kept in hospital, a safe and neutral environment, until it could be established that home was a safe place for them.

There was nothing unusual in any of these procedures, except for the large number of cases under investigation (a result of a long period when there had been staff shortages in the pediatric department – and a growing awareness of the problem of childhood sexual abuse).

A crisis quickly evolved – for the hospital, social services, and police. Somebody had to be blamed. Local church leaders, politicians, and media came together with distressed or dissenting parents, lawyers, and police in a campaign under the slogan, "Give us back our children." To this group of people, the culprits were Drs. Higgs and Wyatt, not the perpetrators of child sexual abuse. The hospital authorities even asked the pediatricians to reduce the number of sexual abuse admissions, as though they had an option of turning away such cases. Following a judicial enquiry, Dr. Higgs was transferred to a different hospital. Both doctors were banned from handling any child abuse work.

When Christ chose to live in solidarity with the poor and the needy in his day, he made himself vulnerable as they were vulnerable; in choosing to be like them, he chose them as his family. The doctors who risked their reputations and careers, and who were publicly vilified, made themselves vulnerable by their actions. They had chosen right relationship with the youngsters, and therefore also with the Holy One. The doctors behaved in accord with the ethical demands of the gospel, and thereby contributed to the ushering in of the reign of Christ.

A decade later some of the children, now young adults, found their own voices to tell what had happened to them in their childhood, and spoke out in support of Drs. Higgs and Wyatt.

Being judged by Christ means being judged by those we know have been abused, whether we have intervened to bring about justice and healing or whether we have been indifferent to their plight. This is not intended as motivation for doing the right thing, but is a consequence of being called to live in right relation to others and to the Holy One. It is a consequence of following the gospel imperative to love one another as Christ loves us.

A peculiar position is given to those of us who have been abused – the position of standing alongside Christ in judgment of the bystanders who either knew what was happening to us when we were young, or who know now what happened. We are not the Christ, but we have a place in the community of faith to exercise power, including the power to judge. This position gives us a responsibility, not as something we choose, but rather as something bestowed upon us by the Divine.

When we disclose abuse and are not taken seriously, we pass judgment when we curtail relationship with those who choose not to believe us, and seek out other people to hear and believe. We pass judgment when we raise our children differently from the way we were raised and break the legacy of family violence. We pass judgment when we refuse to be silenced again, and when we call our abusers to account.

On the other hand, when we disclose abuse and are taken seriously, we pass judgment when the relationship with those who believe us deepens. We pass judgment when we trust some more and share the difficult process of healing. We pass judgment when we celebrate in community the signs that the impact of abuse on our lives is lessening.

We pass judgment when we say "Thank you" to everyone who hears us and believes us, laments and suffers with us, and rises with us in freedom and joy.

◇◇◇◇◇

O living, dancing, judging Presence:
You are there
    in screaming frenzy and flailing limbs
    of little ones
stripped of innocence and trust.
You summon me to enter the fray.

You are there
    in endless sobbing and wordless rage
    of young women and men
abused twenty years ago.
You call me to hear them into speech.

You are there
    in broken stories and wretched grief
    of friend and stranger
    piecing together the past.
You expect me to be a fair witness.

You are always there,
    wherever there is trouble
    daring to touch beauty
    wherever there is separation
    reaching out to link arms
    wherever there is life
    breaking down the prison doors.

You are there
    asking me
    will I be there too,
to receive your blessing?

◇◇◇◇◇

Questions to ask ourselves

- Are there times when I have been indifferent to people who have told me they were sexually abused when they were children?
- How have I responded as honest witness, rather than as passive bystander, to disclosures of abuse?
- Have I ever felt I was taking a risk by believing that someone had been abused?
- In what ways do I pass judgment on people who are indifferent or dismiss me when I am distressed and ask for help?
- Who do I know to be an honest witness to my distress, or grief, or pain? How do I pass judgment on them?

Learning to pray together

Jesus was praying in a certain place, and after he had finished, one of his disciples said to him, "Lord, teach us to pray, as John taught his disciples." He said to them, "When you pray, say:

Our Father in heaven, hallowed be your name.

Your kingdom come.

Give us each day our daily bread.

And forgive us our sins,

for we ourselves forgive everyone indebted to us.

And do not bring us to the time of trial."

LUKE 11:1-4

For many of us brought up in the Christian tradition, the prayer that Jesus taught his disciples – the Lord's Prayer – is one of the first passages from scripture we learn. By hearing it week after week in church and at Sunday school, and perhaps by saying it with parents at home, we learn not only the words but also the special significance of the prayer. If the prayer's petitions are not explained we interpret them for ourselves as best we can.

For an increasing number of people today, though, the prayer gets off to a bad start by addressing the Divine as "Our Father." Even those who find "father" a positive, helpful metaphor admit that it has limitations. No single word or image is ever sufficient to describe the Divine in all fullness. Those of us who have been sexually abused by our fathers have an additional struggle. Why would we choose a word that has connotations of pain and fear to call on one who is about beauty and truth? If we can, we cope with the discrepancy by maintaining two separate meanings for the word father, one for in our prayers in church, the other for in our beds at home. But what if we can't? What if the pain and the fear associated with one context are carried over into the context of prayer?

Jesus used the word *Abba*, translated "Father," to denote an intimate rela-tionship with the Creator. Maybe the less formal word, "Daddy," is a better translation. The intent of "Our Father" at the beginning of the Lord's Prayer is to claim a similar intimacy with the Creator for ourselves. That is no problem if we have healthy and life-giving experiences of intimacy. But what if we don't? Intellectually at least, we might be able to respect from afar the truth and goodness of a Creator called Father. However, emotionally and even physically, we flinch at the suggestion of calling that same Creator Daddy. How can words that either make us flinch or keep the Divine at a safe distance allow us the kind of intimacy Jesus wanted us to have?

The church has a responsibility to foster relationships of intimacy with the Divine. All its teachings, doctrines, procedures, policies, hymns, liturgies, Bible studies, and good works are useless if they fail to convey in meaningful ways the love, the mystery, and the glory of the Divine. The church has to listen as well as speak; it has to learn as well as teach; it has to risk facing evil in order to set people free.

It is not uncommon for abused children to become very loyal to their abusers, indeed almost to worship them. Children believe, rightly or wrongly, that if they protect and care for their abusers, they are also doing all they can to protect and care for themselves. Abusers hold all the power. They are the ones to be obeyed at all costs. They are the ones on whom little children depend to stay alive. Not surprisingly, then, an abuser can even usurp the Divine in the mind of an abused child. When that happens the words sung, spoken, and prayed in church can take on a very different meaning – as in the following interpretation.

◇◇◇◇◇

Our Father, who art in Heaven, hallowed be thy name.
> I must worship my father, Daddy the boss,
>> who lives in his own place,
>> his study, his bedroom, his house.
> Protect his name.
> Be loyal to him before anyone else
>> if I don't want to die.

Thy kingdom come, thy will be done, on earth as it is Heaven.
> Always, no matter what, I must let him have his way.
> Do what he says: no noise, no telling.
> Forget – if I can.
> If he wants me naked, so be it.
> If he wants me tied up, so be it.
> If he wants me drugged, so be it.
> If he wants me alone, so be it.
> If he wants me to watch while he rapes another child, so be it.
> If he wants me in his room or my room,
>> on the kitchen table or on the altar at church, so be it.
> Let him have his way, whenever, wherever, however he wants it.
> He is the king who rules my body
>> and controls my mind with threats of death.

Give us this day our daily bread.
> He will feed me what he says I deserve:
>> semen, excrement, secrets and lies.
> Eat it all up. Don't gag or vomit.

Forgive us our trespasses as we forgive them that trespass against us.

    Daddy, I'm sorry.

    I didn't mean it whatever it was I said or did

        or thought or am to make you so angry.

    I won't do it again, whatever it is.

    I promise. I mean it. I am so bad.

    I have nothing to forgive, for you are always right.

    You are the boss, the king.

Lead us not into temptation, but deliver us from evil.

    Never for one instant think I can change the way things are.

    Remember what happens when I resist him:

    Ropes pulled tighter when I struggle to be free;

        the knife at my throat when I scream out in pain.

    Only Daddy can keep me alive.

    He knows how much pain I can bear.

    He's there to comfort me when the drugs wear off.

    His hypnotic voice lulls me to sleep after he's done.

For thine is the kingdom, the power and the glory, forever and ever. Amen.

    Don't question his command or undermine his power.

    He is always right.

    Dispense with truth, and feeling, and hope.

    Pledge allegiance to him and him alone,

        who is supreme,

        yesterday, today and tomorrow.

    So be it.

This reworking of the Lord's Prayer serves to emphasize the enormous power that an abuser has over a child. It raises the question of how the church relates to people who have been so badly hurt that a part of them truly believes and lives by the thoughts expressed above. We can learn by listening to how a different part of an abused person might relate to the Divine.

Holy One,
> who is always there to welcome me
> when I can bear the pain no more,
> how safe it is to be with you.

You ask no questions,
> you make no demands,
> for you already know why I am here.

You know what I need, and give it freely:
> rest, comfort and love.

You hold me close and wait with me,
> bearing my sadness,
> watching with me…

While he hurts my body,
> and controls my mind.

Holy One,
> I could not bear it alone.

By grace, I know your greater power,
> and learn your holy way of love.

By grace, despair is reborn as hope.

You have never failed me, and never will.

◇◇◇◇◇

The church will be a help rather than a hindrance to individuals healing from child sexual abuse when it addresses the difficulties that its liturgies and practices unwittingly present. We only begin to do this by looking more closely at some of the assumptions that lie behind the use of the Lord's Prayer. Thankfully, many churches now use a variety of words and images, and not only Father. The New Zealand Book of Common Prayer, for example, begins one version of the Lord's Prayer with "Eternal Spirit, Earth-maker, Pain-bearer, Life-giver, Source of all that is, Father and Mother of us all." Everybody benefits from changes such as this. Prayers once said by rote come alive in new ways.

Our understanding of heaven is related to the name(s) we use for the Divine. The church has traditionally thought of heaven as a physical place, a kingdom somewhere up in the sky, very different from earth. In this kingdom, an omnipotent, omniscient divine being lives and rules. The time is now ripe for this model of heaven and its king to be set aside as part of the church's bric-a-brac of former times.

Instead, we can attend to the model that Jesus gave. By his teachings and his vulnerability, Jesus showed that heaven is a particular way of being, present to us here and now, rather than a remote place we might attain in the future. In my experience, the uncertainty of a distant time and place, and the uncertainty of ever getting there, are not helpful to people struggling to come to terms with the ugly realities they have had to endure. They need reassurance and comfort now.

The church's teaching about forgiveness has generally been two-fold. First we must confess our own wrongdoing in order to be forgiven. Secondly, we must be willing to forgive anyone who has wronged us. This would seem to be in accord with the line, "forgive us our trespasses as we forgive them that trespass against us."

In the context of a close-knit faith community such as the one Luke first addressed in his gospel it is possible to imagine a milieu of openness, understanding, and mutual forgiveness. The context of a family in which

the violence and deceit of child sexual abuse are concealed is very different. What if we don't – because we can't – forgive those who have wronged
us? Elsewhere in the gospels there are calls for repentance as a prerequisite
for forgiveness. When abusers refuse to acknowledge what they have done
wrong, let alone seek to turn their lives around, or to take responsibility for
the long-lasting harm their actions caused, a strong case can be made for not
forgiving. Indeed, perhaps that is the more faithful action to take.

As the church works to dismantle the barriers between itself and the
needs of broken people longing for wholeness we all move a little closer to
being able to pray together in ways that are faithful to the whole of Jesus'
teachings, and to right relationship with our Creator.

◇◇◇◇◇

Our Father, who art in Heaven, hallowed be thy name.
> Holy One,
> Creator of the universe,
> Source of life and love, laughter and trust,
>> in you is all goodness, beauty and truth.
> Let everything that is, sing out your name with joy.

Thy kingdom come, thy will be done, on earth as it is Heaven.
> You bless us with freedom to determine our own path,
>> yet you are always with us when we stumble and fall.
> May our desires be born of love.
> May our lives answer your longing for peace.

Give us this day our daily bread.

> Your gift to us of bread each day
> comes from earth and air, water and sun.
> Let us live in such a way that your giving is never thwarted,
> and so that all may receive.

Forgive us our trespasses as we forgive them that trespass against us.

> You share the pain that we inflict out of ignorance, fear and greed.
> Forgive us for hurting one another and your creation.
> Open our hearts to welcome those who seek forgiveness from us.
> Receive into your care those we cannot forgive.

Lead us not into temptation, but deliver us from evil.

> Keep us from working our own revenge.
> Increase our courage to use our power for love.
> Strengthen us to resist the temptation to be more than, or less than, you
> have made us.
> And deliver us from evil.

For thine is the kingdom, the power and the glory, forever and ever. Amen.

> Since the beginning of time, love has been your realm.
> The only power that matters is the power of love.
> Wherever there is love, you are there.
> Glory be to you forever.
> Amen.

◇◇◇◇◇

Questions to ask ourselves

- To whom did I pray as a little child?
- Are there words or images for the Divine used in church that get in the way of my ability to pray? How do I react to them?
- What words or images do I prefer to use when I pray?
- What does heaven mean to me?
- Do I stumble over any of the petitions in the Lord's Prayer, such as the ones that concern forgiveness or evil? What do I need to pray instead?

Part 3

Life

A letter to Bartimaeus

They came to Jericho. As he and his disciples and a large crowd were leaving Jericho, Bartimaeus son of Timaeus, a blind beggar, was sitting by the roadside. When he heard that it was Jesus of Nazareth, he began to shout out and say, "Jesus, Son of David, have mercy on me!" Many sternly ordered him to be quiet, but he cried out even more loudly, "Son of David, have mercy on me!" Jesus stood still and said, "Call him here." And they called the blind man saying to him, "Take heart; get up, he is calling you." So throwing off his cloak, he sprang up and came to Jesus. Then Jesus said to him, "What do you want me to do for you?" The blind man said to him, "My teacher, let me see again." Jesus said to him, "Go; your faith has made you well." Immediately, he regained his sight and followed him on the way.

MARK 10:46-52

My dear Bartimaeus:

Writing to you after all these years is like writing to an old friend; it's almost as though I have known you my whole life. I am so glad of that, so glad to be able to count you among the significant people who have been with me, stood by me, and kept a lookout for me on this long, long journey. Though you know as well as anyone that I haven't always felt this way. When I was first introduced to you I hardly noticed you, and certainly didn't recognize you as someone who might be important to me. Since that first unmemorable meeting I must have heard your story another hundred times – you, the blind beggar sitting by the roadside, whom Jesus healed. And every time I heard it I thought to myself either "So what?" or "Yeah, right! As if!"

On the face of it I always found the story of how you got your sight back somewhat bland, and not much different from all the other healing stories that had gone before it. What did it have to do with the piece in scripture that it comes right after, the piece where the disciples have a big fight over who is most important and Jesus gets mad with them all for being so dumb and not seeing what really matters? It was too easy then to skip over your story and on to some more excitement, on to the account of Jesus' magnificent entry into Jerusalem. And anyway, how could you expect me to believe your story? I didn't know of any healings like yours taking place in my lifetime. The only way I knew people could recover their sight was through eye transplants or laser eye surgery, which nobody had dreamt of when you were healed.

Of course, now when I look back to my first responses of indifference and cynicism, I can see I was unconsciously protecting myself, and hiding from the truth of my own need for healing. I had managed to get by, faking wellness for so long, that you had a lot of resistance to overcome to reach me. That resistance didn't come only from myself and all the different parts of me, it came from other people too – my family, my friends, and even my enemies. None of us was willing to listen to what you had to say, no matter how good your intentions. We simply weren't prepared to deal with the chaos that would ensue.

Resistance to you, Bartimaeus, and to your story takes so many forms. It's strange that today, when health care is such a priority in our social system, we still resist healing. Much of it is fear of change, and I'm sure you remember about that. After all, at least when you were a blind beggar you knew what was expected of you and every day was more or less predictable. I don't mean to downplay the humiliation of having to sit and beg for food on the road at the edge of town, but you had done it for so long you knew what your role in life was, you knew how to fit in, you knew how to get people to tolerate you even if they didn't particularly like you. People needed you to stay the way you were, though of course they wouldn't admit it. They needed to be able to pray, "Thank you, God, that we aren't blind like that poor beggar Bartimaeus. Thank you that we earn our living through an honest day's work, and not from begging like Bartimaeus." They needed you so they could say to one another, "I wonder what he did wrong to deserve his fate." They needed you, poor and blind, a down-and-out nobody, so they could believe their wealth and status proved they were somebodies.

As for me, I also knew what was expected of me. The members of my own family, who had known me all my life, expected me and needed me never to tell about being sexually abused, and never to show my feelings. Over time, this spread to other people too. For 30 years I kept the "secret." Few people ever saw me angry or afraid, excited or bored, happy or sad. I grew up being emotionally flat except on those rare occasions when some little thing would make me laugh hysterically or cry uncontrollably for hours. Then I felt alive, though the intensity was alarming and I wasn't sorry to feel very little most of the time. When I was young I always sensed I was different from other children; I acted very independent, but felt very needy. It seemed this would never change and it came to define who I was, just as being blind defined who you were, Bartimaeus. Looking back I now know that what I most needed was to feel loved. My show of independence was a way of hiding this need and avoiding rejection. Once, a favorite teacher momentarily held my face between her hands as a sign that she was proud of me as a student. I wanted so badly to believe this gesture meant she loved me, I used to recall the sensation of her soft hands on my cheeks many, many times.

Later on, when I was no longer a child, my life didn't seem that bad. I had a place to live, a job I liked, and my own two children who drove me crazy although I wouldn't have traded them for the world. There was little motivation for me to make any shift in my life, or in my perspective on life. I was quietly and comfortably resigned to wait for certain significant people to see me for who I really was – kind, good, and lovable. I just had to wait long enough and they would be overwhelmed by the evidence. It didn't matter that they, my parents, had chosen to hurt me and neglect me; it didn't matter that everyone was in enormous denial about this, including me; it didn't matter that from time to time I spiraled down into feelings of absolute worthlessness. I just had to hope harder for them to change. Eventually they would love me.

That's where I was stuck when your story first had an impact on me. You came to me suddenly like a traveler through space and time to show me a better way. You showed me that if I was ever going to heal I had to give up hope of other people changing. Give up hope of them coming around. Give up the dream that had made life seem worthwhile. Give up the dream that I had relied on for as long as I could remember.

So I resisted you – again. But this time I couldn't shut you out. Although I heard myself say in a loud voice, "No," deeper down inside I heard another voice say, "Yes. Listen to Bartimaeus." You and I talked then about hope and the importance – sometimes – of waiting without hope. As T. S. Eliot wrote in *The Four Quartets*, "Wait without hope for hope would be for the wrong thing." We also talked about a scene in one of Elie Wiesel's novels where two refugees are fleeing for their lives from some soldiers. They can hear the soldiers speaking. They can even see the light from their flashlights reflecting off the trees. And they have to make a run for it. One of the refugees asks, "What if there is no hope?" To which the other replies, "Never mind, we'll get by without it."

Giving up hope of specific things, waiting without hope, getting by without hope: When I finally did let go of hope, it was like stepping over the edge and going beyond what my reality had been until then. Who would have thought that hope of all things would be the last layer of scab to be removed before the festering abscess would finally burst and healing could begin?

You stepped over the edge, Bartimaeus. You behaved like a madman when you started screaming, "Jesus, son of David, have mercy on me." You cast aside who you had been when you jumped up, threw off your cloak, and ran to Jesus. And having come that far, you weren't about to compromise when he asked you what you wanted him to do. I mean, you could have said, "Let me see just a little," or you could have said, "Make my life a little easier." But no. You kept on going the whole way and asked for it all. "Give me my sight please."

Perhaps it was your absolute confidence and single-mindedness that reached into me and demanded my attention. For when I felt the connection between us, sheer determination swept over me. I found myself insisting on no half-measures, no more band-aid cures, no cautious approach to the Holy One who heals. I found myself in an unavoidable head-on collision with Truth, that was both desperate and right. I realized with utter clarity what I needed most of all. Rather than needing other people to regard me as good and lovable, I needed to regard myself that way.

Instead of asking for more loving friends, or for a devoted and loving life partner, or for just one of my parents to show me his or her love, I found myself standing in front of the Holy One completely open and vulnerable. I had shed my protective independence and denial of the past. I was fully present to reality and truth. I accepted what I saw: that I was – and am – a child of the divine Creator, and a sister of Jesus. I uncovered the fact that I am basically good, and lovable, and yes, even loved.

Having once seen this truth I could no longer return to the way things used to be, any more than you could continue being a blind beggar once you had received your sight. You immediately made the decision to follow Jesus on his way; you didn't indulge in the countless possibilities that opened up for you once you could see. You took hold of the new responsibility that came with being a whole person instead of a pitiful beggar who could do so little for himself and even less for other people.

I confess when I first saw my truth I was tempted to indulge in retribution and revenge. I wanted to say to people, "Look at me, there is nothing wrong with me after all. You are the ones who are sick. You are the ones who are truly in need." Then when I calmed down a little I was tempted to say, "Let me tell you what happened to me, so that you too can be healed." I was glad of your example, Bartimaeus, glad that you modeled the importance of simply following Jesus, who still had much to teach you and show you.

Over the years since I first truly encountered your story and the gospel story infused within it, I have come to realize that faith not only *makes* us well, faith also *keeps* us well. This is the mystery of faith – that when we follow, when we see, when we dare to love and know goodness, then our seeing and loving are refined and enriched. We learn to be more fully ourselves. We learn to do more completely what is right. Faith compels us to follow ever more closely the way that leads to the Source of all goodness, truth, beauty, and love.

Bartimaeus, my friend, I will always remember you with enormous gratitude, and whenever I can I will tell people what a difference you made to my life. Is it possible that all our stories together will one day heal the whole world, and all Creation will once again be seen to be very, very good? This is my longing, this is my prayer. This is my reason for following my brother Jesus.

◇◇◇◇◇

Questions to ask ourselves

- Have I ever felt cynical about or indifferent towards the significance of a person's healing?
- When I read scripture, am I open to the possibility of transformation?
- How have I resisted healing? (for example: by minimizing the pain, by denying anything bad has ever happened, by filling up my life with distractions, by misusing alcohol or drugs)
- What am I hoping for?
- When I contemplate giving up hope – in the sense of emptying myself to the present moment – what thoughts and feelings come to mind?
- What do I need now to take the next step on my journey towards wholeness?
- Do I ever feel self-righteous because of healing that has occurred in my life?
- When I reread the passage Mark 10:46-52, what is my prayer?

Departing from evil

"Where then does wisdom come from?
   And where is the place of understanding?
It is hidden from the eyes of all living,
   and concealed from the birds of the air.
Abaddon and Death say,
   'We have heard a rumor of it with our ears.'
"God understands the way to it,
   and he knows its place.
For he looks to the ends of the earth,
   and sees everything under the heavens.
When he gave to the wind its weight,
   and apportioned out the waters by measure;
when he made a decree for the rain,
   and a way for the thunderbolt;
then he saw it and declared it;
   he established it, and searched it out.
And he said to humankind,
   'Truly, the fear of the Lord, that is wisdom;
   and to depart from evil is understanding.'"

JOB 28:20-28

Human suffering and the problem of evil, the meaning of true friendship and the nature of God – these are just a few of the many themes woven into the book of Job. The suffering of the innocent is perhaps the theme of most interest to those abused as children, but the other themes cannot be ignored, for they are all interconnected. Likewise it is difficult to select any one passage without reading it in the context of the whole book. So although the text selected for this reflection is a beautiful and rich piece of poetry, its full worth is only seen when the urgency of the initial questions about wisdom and understanding is appreciated.

The book of Job opens with a wager between God and Satan, and closes with clear evidence as to who has won. The wager has to do with "how to talk about God." The upright and innocent man Job has always spoken well of God, but in the heavenly court Satan maintains that this is only because Job has always had a comfortable life. Job has enjoyed prosperity, protection, and blessings on all his undertakings. Satan's position is that Job would not be so good and devout if he were to lose all the things that are dear to him; God believes that Job's devotion is disinterested and not in any way manipulative. God agrees to prove this position by testing Job.

When Job loses his children and his possessions he still does not turn away from God. In a second stage of testing, Job becomes ill; his whole body is covered in ulcers. But still Job does not curse God for what has befallen him.

Job's friends explain to him that his misfortunes and sudden ill health must be divine punishment for some terrible sins that he has committed, yet Job knows himself to be innocent. His wife, who suffers with him the loss of children and possessions, urges him to stop being so stubborn, to stop speaking well of God in the face of such tragedy. Better, she says, to curse God and die. Still Job continues to speak faithfully. Not that he is silent about his situation. He does curse the day he was born. Because of his suffering he regards the universe as essentially chaotic and empty of holiness. Paradoxically though, the raw power of Job's lament gives profound expression of his hope and ultimate surrender to his Creator.

God's response to Job does not directly answer his questions, and certainly does not offer an explanation or a justification for his suffering. Instead, it exposes the limitations of Job's efforts to understand God and his desire to define God only in terms of his own suffering. The nature of the Holy One surpasses the imagination of a suffering man. When Job understands this he realizes that his own identity also surpasses his suffering. Yes, he suffers, but his connection with the Holy is not limited by his suffering.

Perhaps the questions Job was asking cannot be answered, and yet it was essential that he asked them. At the time they were the only way he knew how to talk to God; better to articulate his concerns and invoke a conversation with God than to turn aside. Better to ask questions that might embrace less than the whole truth about the Holy One and the Universe, and listen for answers, than refrain from both asking and listening and so absent oneself from the relationship. When God speaks, the miracle is that Job's faith is deepened and his perspective on his suffering is dramatically shifted.

If through our own suffering we identify with the troubled Job, we will hear an invitation to enter into the mystery of relationship with our Creator. If we accept the invitation we relinquish all simplistic answers and instead commit ourselves to integrity and truth. We risk having our eyes opened to the shallowness of people who mean well; we risk transformation by the Holy One whose thoughts are not our thoughts and whose ways are not our ways. We have to give up our preconceived ideas about ourselves and our world, and our place in the world. We will find a new place in which to worship the Creator of all that is.

◇◇◇◇◇

1.

Holy of holies

    as people who were hurt in childhood

        we bring you our questions, complaints and yes, our accusations,

even though when our so-called friends overhear us

    they will rush in to defend you and their own position

        with worn-out arguments

            that they think will set us straight.

2.
Our friends offer their sympathy and understanding.
    Giving us something makes them feel better about our plight.
But for us their well-meaning platitudes miss the mark.
We are unwilling recipients of patronizing consolation.

Our friends say that we must have been the first to sin.
We must have tempted the grownups into trespassing on our bodies
    by being too lovely not to touch or
        by being too curious in our innocence or
            by being pure and perfect
and therefore just right and ripe for the taking.

Our friends say that our abusers were sick;
    and that is sufficient explanation for our suffering.
If only we could give up wallowing in our pain
    then we would understand its cause and healing would follow.

Our friends say it didn't really happen;
    we are victims instead of unscrupulous therapists
        putting ideas into our heads
    and images of violation into our dreams.
Their neo-Freudian speech keeps them safe –
    it denies the truth and adds to our frustration.

Our friends say we could keep a more balanced view.
Why not remember all the good things, such as food and shelter,
    instead of only remembering the bad?
Then benefits could cancel out harm
    and our suffering would be relieved.

3.

Our friends talk on and on *about* the Holy One.

We want instead to talk *to* the Holy One.

We want to protest our innocence to our Creator,

    for nothing we did as little children

    merited the suffering we still endure.

Not the sweets we stole, not the clothes we soiled;

    not the lies we told, not the mean things we said;

    not the shoves and pushes we used to get ahead,

    not our crying by night for comfort

    not our misery by day for love withheld.

When we were children we had to keep silent.

Now, O Holy One, we have a choice.

Now, we are finding our voices;

Will we who suffered remember or forget?

Will we demand of you, the Creator of the Universe, real answers,

    or will we keep hidden what never should have been?

Will we be accomplices of our own abusers and let them stay free,

    or will we tell of their crimes and turn them in?

Why, O Holy One, did you not speak up for us?

Where were you then, when they controlled our world?

Where are you now, now that our world is out of control?

Why have we been sentenced to years of anguish

    while they are not even summoned to a trial?

Will you still keep silent and ignore our plea?

4.

Look, the people whose wickedness stole our innocence
    flourish in a world deaf to our cries.
An abusive priest is known about town
    for his concern for the poor and oppressed.
A doctor who misused drugs on his own sons
    is famous for his play therapy with pre-school children.
A Sunday school teacher respected by her church
    recruits young children for her pedophile friend.
A lawyer who offered his niece as a sex-slave
    is a popular advocate for refugees.

Holy God of Justice,
    do you not see, do you not care
        that your ways are being perverted
        that your commandments are forgotten
        that your creation is filled with rampant violation
            of the most vulnerable?

Holy God of Wisdom,
    stop listening to our friends for they have it all wrong.
Their sympathy is too shallow, their understanding null and void,
    for we never asked to be hurt,
    we never invited suffering upon ourselves.
The good that we knew doesn't undo the bad;
    our all too frequent nightmares have their basis in truth.
Whatever the cause, whatever the disease that laid waste our lives,
    we still hurl our question, "Where were you?"

5.

Intellectual verbiage offers us no comfort –
    not that comfort is what we seek most.
Rather, give us the reason for our belief.
How can we cling fast to hope
    when such chaos and disorder abound?
Is the only way to wisdom through our afflictions
    instead of a rescue from our afflictions?
Is understanding found in the very act of prayer
    instead of in the answer to prayer?

6.

We too must stop listening to our friends.
Wisdom is well hidden from their eyes.
We must end our obsession with the prosperity of the wicked.
It does not help us to understand.

Our only help will come from the Holy One,
    maker of heaven and earth,
    who created all things out of the chaos of the deep.
Is the Holy One not more than our pain?
Does wisdom not exceed the limits of our imagination?
Even in these times the mystery of the Universe
    is not fully defined by scientific laws.
Revelation is more than mathematical formulation;
    our sense of wonder is indeed beyond measure.

O Great Creator, to you we would pray

　　mindful of your freedom to call wind and rain, sea and sky into being.

Surely our prayers will not keep us from wisdom.

Surely seeing your freedom cannot lead us astray.

◇◇◇◇◇

7.

Ah, little ones, I have heard your questions, complaints, and accusations.

You do not lie in what you say, yet neither do you tell the whole truth.

You do not lie when you say what happened was wrong and undeserved.

Nothing children ever do merits using and hurting them for selfish pleasure.

Yet you leave out the fact that I did not abandon you.

Even your friends know I was with you,

　　but they misunderstand.

I was not with you to scold you or punish you,

　　or even because you called me.

I was there of my own free will

　　to suffer with you what you could not bear alone.

You called to heaven that I come down and rescue,

when all the time I was close beside you,

　　knowing with you the injustice and the pain.

Just as surely as I make the wind to blow across the prairie

　　and the waves to lap against the shore,

　　　just as surely as I set the stars to spin and dance in the heavens

　　　so I keep company with all the little ones on earth

　　　for your agony and rage are also mine.

Your prayers travel no distance before reaching my ears.

Your innocent cries join the wailing of my own voice.

Your tears mingle with mine.

Your surrender to me is a holy undertaking.

When you asked, "Where were you, Holy One?"

　　you looked only to the heavens for your answer.

When you asked, "Why did it happen?"

　　you tuned your ear to human reason alone.

The shouting of your questions

　　made you deaf to my small voice within;

Your frantic searching for answers

　　made you blind to my presence before you.

Even now, you are free to hear and see my holy word and way,

　　or to turn aside in pride and self-righteousness.

The freedom I have to speak and to act as I will is also yours.

I have no desire, nor power even, to force you to make my way your own.

When you turn your face to mine, see! I've been here all the time.

When you listen for my voice, hear! I've been calling you forever.

Stay a while and know that you are mine and I am yours.

Drink from the Source of Life.

Rest in the shade of my goodness.

You will know when you are ready to journey on some more,

　　and when you do you will know I travel with you.

You will know we go together to wherever injustice must be overcome

　　and wherever little ones are crying out for peace.

◇◇◇◇◇

8.

Holy One,

  we remember when we very young

you were with us in the times of terror,

  rocking us against your breast,

  murmuring to us your lullaby of peace.

We remember leaving our bodies in the hands of our abusers

  and flying away to be with you.

You were our refuge and our strength;

  you were our only safety in those long nights.

Then we had no questions for you;

We knew you to be our answer.

But now is different.

Now you have heard us question your wisdom

  and seen our indignant search for understanding.

Now you are breaking into our prison,

  snapping the bars we had reinforced with fear and shame.

When we first cried out our adult grief

  we did not remember who you were.

We abandoned you when we listened for your Word

  only in the speech of our friends.

We neglected the vastness of your creation

  and your intervention throughout all space and time.

Now, when we recall your presence with us long ago

  we ache at the knowledge of wounds scored deep within.

The pain we sought to escape is all too fresh;

  the suffering we hoped to skim over demands our full attention.

This we also know, that still today
    young children continue to be hurt.
Human freedom is nonaligned with yours.
Goodness does not yet prevail.

But let us gather all our courage together
    and pledge allegiance to your holy way.
Let our struggle be not only for ourselves.
Through our prayers make us to understand your will for us,
    and having suffered our own pain
        let us recommit to relieve that of others.
Let us know you in every movement towards life
    and see you in every sacred gesture.
Let us hear you in every word of healing,
    and touch you in every hand of love.

Because having come this far
    we will never let you go.
You are ours, and we are yours.
You are the Source of Life;
    whatever flows from you brings redemption to the world.
With you we will travel on.
We will never let you go.

◇◇◇◇◇

Questions to ask ourselves

- How do I talk about the Divine, given the suffering in my life?
- Do I believe that I must have done something wrong to deserve being hurt as a child?
- Is it my fault that I continue to feel the painful effects of what was done to me as a child?
- What advice do my friends offer? Is it always helpful?
- Do I need to understand all the reasons for the hurt inflicted on me before I can heal?
- How do I describe the presence of the Holy One with me when I pray?
- Where do I find wisdom?

Reckless faith

For the promise that he would inherit the world did not come to Abraham or to his descendants through the law but through the righteousness of faith.

ROMANS 4:13

O Creator, I read your promise to Abraham, that he will "inherit the world," and I wonder if you make the same promise to all people of faith. Specifically, I wonder if you promise me a world where I know I belong.

Do you promise a physical place of country, town, and home that is safe? Do you promise a social place of family, community, and society that acknowledges and understands the impact of severe trauma on a child? Do you promise an emotional place of respect, and mutuality, and love? Do you promise a spiritual place of gratitude and deep connection with you, my Creator?

Perhaps you do. Sometimes I believe you do. But what must I do, O Holy One, to make your promise come true?

This is what I am doing. I go to therapy, week after week, month after month, year after year. I confront my abusers, and the people who knew but did nothing to help me. I tell the police, the church, and the professional organization that my abuser belongs to. I strive to understand why people do terrible things to children. I teach my own children how to keep themselves safe, and the importance of telling right away if ever someone hurts them. I work so hard at healing, yet your promised land remains elusive. Nothing I do makes right what was wrong. Nothing I do saves me from the past.

Help me, Holy One, to know and accept my limitations. How I want to be in control of everything that happens, as if to make up for all those years when I had no control! Cure me of the notion that I am able to make myself whole, that I have that amount of power. Surely I cannot save myself. I cannot keep your promise for you. I can never do enough. Yet this I ask – increase my faith so that I believe enough.

Without a connection to you, Holy One, doubt and despair threaten to overwhelm me. In your absence the mad compulsion that I must somehow

save myself becomes an unworthy touchstone and guide. I struggle to understand how my abuser could belong to the same faith community as so
many good people. I struggle to feel at home in myself, to feel good about
being human. But having witnessed the evil that human beings do, I want
to escape my own humanity.

I have heard it said that you are able to set the world right, and if only I
had faith I would see myself set right within it. But in what can I hope when
I have no faith? On what power can I depend when I cannot even pray?

I remember one night when an old, deeply buried sense of outright indignation arose within me to fill every fiber and cell of my being. The injustice
of what had been done to me was before me like a fathomless cliff face; there
were no handholds or footholds to help break it down into manageable steps;
there was no possible route by which it could be scaled. It demanded my
attention yet at the same time reduced me to powerlessness. I could neither
surmount it, nor turn from it. I had to be with it, unbearable as that was.
Worse, I could not even pray, for it seemed prayer would distract or diminish its significance. I couldn't afford any room for faith, yet miraculously I
found help in the faith of the church. In desperation I flung myself in the
path of the prayers and petitions of others, and hitched my longing on to
theirs. Shortly afterwards, a surprising measure of comfort and peace came
to me. Since that night I have often known the blessing of a community of
faith that is praying without ceasing, that mercifully carries our yearning to
the Source of all Life.

◇◇◇◇◇

For this reason it depends on faith, in order that the promise may rest on grace...
and be guaranteed to all who share the faith.

Romans 4:16

Holy One,
    now is not a good time,
    now is not a time of peace,
      or hope or joy or love.

Now is a time of rage and grief.
Now is a time of terror and pain.
Now is a time I want to end very soon;
I cannot endure any more.

This has lasted long enough.
Where is your mercy since I have no hope?
Where is your love since I do not know it?
Where is your grace which invokes a new day?

"Have faith," they say, mocking my cries.
"What is now is not forever;
    just wait and see."

I want nothing to do with them;
I don't believe what they say is true.

My faith in you is like that of a fool:
Although this time might be forever,
    by faith in you I will outlast it.
Although hope has escaped my grasp,
    by faith in you I will get by without hope.

Although grace which once surprised me
>> is now known only by its absence
>> yet I do know it.
By faith, grace will return.

Holy One,
>> now is not a good time,
>> now is not a time of peace,
>>> or hope or joy or love.

Now is the time to hurl myself with reckless faith at you.
All I can lose is grief and despair.
All I can gain is known only to you.

◇◇◇◇◇

No distrust made him waver concerning the promise of God.

ROMANS 4:20

O Holy One, who has made all things, who desires all things to live in harmony and peace: I bring before you the unrest that disturbs my peace, I bring you the chaos out of which harmony has yet to be fashioned. I bring you my brokenness and in my mind's eye a plan you can use to make me whole.

My plan is this. First, you forgive me for all the times I couldn't find the words, the language, the sounds to let people know the pain and distress that my abusers caused me. Forgive me all the times I have not been able to trust. Of course, nobody could help if I did not trust them enough to tell them what was wrong. Then – after you have forgiven me – you teach me how to trust. If you carry out my plan I will be healed. If you carry out my plan, your promise of a better future will be fulfilled.

I wait expectantly.

Almost immediately I sense your presence, and I truly believe you are here to do what I ask. But no! In one quick sweep of your hand you brush aside my plan for wholeness. Sooner than I can reach to rescue what you discard, you take hold of me, and your breath whispers through my being:

"Little one,
     there is nothing to forgive, for you did nothing wrong.
You lost your need to trust
     because there was nobody present to honor it.
You learnt well how to live without it,
     relying on your innermost strength,
     and on the faintest of visions of a different way.
Your need to trust became unnecessary, redundant and a burden.
You shed that need like a first skin
     too restrictive for you to grow well.
Now the time has come for you to grieve that loss.

"See, I am giving you a sign:
On the ground before you lies an empty shell.
Take it, hold it, make it your own,
     this gray-brown barnacle-encrusted chiton,
     with turquoise bands lining the inside.
Keep it awhile as a reminder of your first skin,
     as a sign that long ago you lost your need to trust.
It is a beautiful shell, there is no other like it.
What you lost had beauty too, and belonged only to you.
Remember it, grieve it, and I will give you rest.
By your faith in me, I will make you whole."

◇◇◇◇◇

Therefore, since we are justified by faith, we have peace with God through our
Lord Jesus Christ, though whom we have obtained access to this grace.

ROMANS 5:1-2

O Creator,
you are the beginning and the middle and the end of all peace.
When I am right with you
    then I can see all is right with the world.
When I know I belong to you,
    then I know belonging in the world.

Even when the world turns its back on me
    for being too outspoken
        too demanding,
        too truthful,
        too persistent,
        too confrontational,
even then – because I belong to you –
    I am glad to be alive,
    for you surprise me at every turn.

At the dawning of your new day
    I speak out – again –
        my same old complaint,
        but something different is before me.
New ears hear me,
    and I hear for the first time
        shouts of solidarity, friendship, and love.

When I summon a friend of faith
    into the blackest night
    without hesitation he agrees to come.
He lets me show him the worst horrors;
    he flinches but doesn't run,
    he shudders, but doesn't turn away.
When my terror brushes against him
    he moves closer to me.
When distant sounds of merriment call him away
    he embraces me and promises to stay.

When I cry out to you, O Holy One,
    lamenting my suffering,
another friend of faith
    promises to pray for me every day of her life;
    promises to lament and weep,
    and laugh and rejoice with me,
    as long as she is alive.

When I lack words
    to describe the hell I have known
another writes a poem
    pledging accompaniment
    holding me in the shelter of community
    longing for transformation
    shedding warm rays of hope
      on a future filled with love.

The community of Christ pours out your grace.
It dares to know with me the forces of evil
     and is bold to stand with me against them.
The community of Christ knows your mystery.
It aligns itself with the foolishness of faith
     and rejects all fear and self-serving platitudes.
The community of Christ receives your gift of peace.
With open arms we welcome you,
     our holy, vulnerable, inviting Lover.
With open hearts we enter into your joy,
     and one with you we are made whole.

◇◇◇◇◇

Questions to ask ourselves

- In light of my suffering, what would it mean for me to "inherit the world"?
- Are there things I think I must do to ensure God is able to care for me?
- Are there times when my faith has felt empty and I have consciously relied on the faith and prayers of other people?
- When have my faith and prayers been a source of strength to other people?
- Do I feel guilty about my lack of faith, or ashamed when I find it hard to pray? Is my guilt and shame exacerbated by things that were said or done to me when I was a child?
- Am I comfortable with being angry at God? How do I express my anger?
- What have been the landmarks of my journey through grief and sadness over what I lost in childhood? Where am I now on that journey?
- What are some signs of grace and peace in my life?

Weeping and work, joy and coming home

When the Lord restored the fortunes of Zion,
we were like those who dream.
Then our mouth was filled with laughter,
and our tongue with shouts of joy;
then it was said among the nations,
"The Lord has done great things for them."
The Lord has done great things for us,
and we rejoiced.

Restore our fortunes, O Lord,
like the watercourses in the Negeb.
May those who sow in tears
reap with shouts of joy.
Those who go out weeping,
bearing the seed for sowing,
shall come home with shouts of joy,
carrying their sheaves.

PSALM 126

Anyone who has experienced sexual abuse as a child, or is close to someone who has, knows the necessity and the importance of tears. Enduring abuse, healing from it, and accompanying others as they heal, are all undeniably hard work. Weeping is a sign of grief and rage, pain and despair, and eventually of relief. Weeping is a sign of the work that is being done. Our prayer is that one day we will reap the benefits of our labor. If we confront the truth about what has happened, and continues to happen, surely one day it will stop. Surely one day those who have been abused will know wholeness, freedom, and new life.

In this short psalm a worshipping people express their confidence in the Divine to bring about a renewed state of happiness and well-being. Their past experience, when things were not going so well, is that divine intervention eventually brought about a complete change in their fortune. People who had seen their religious center of Jerusalem destroyed, and who had been forced into exile, were able to return to their homeland with hope of rebuilding their city and temple. The psalm does not specify present circumstances. The prayer "restore our fortunes" only suggests that once again the people are having a hard time. However, the overall tenor of the psalm is optimistic. The intercession, "May those who sow in tears reap with shouts of joy" repeats in the following verse as a statement of faith. Their confidence in better times ahead is so great that they can cheerfully sing, "Those who go out with weeping... shall come home with shouts of joy." Whatever the details of the present crisis, the people can look back and remember that previous hard times did not last forever. Just as then, so now. Soon, all will be well.

For a people whose livelihood is derived from growing and harvesting crops, sowing seeds is work, work without instant gratification, but – in the fullness of time – seeds germinate, plants grow, grain ripens, and crops are harvested. Between sowing and reaping there is a time of patient waiting, a time of faith and hope. The prayer in difficult times is that even if there is grief and sadness while the work of sowing is being carried out, by harvest time tears will be dry and joyful songs will be sung.

◇◇◇◇◇

May those who sow in tears, reap with shouts of joy.

Sometimes it is too easy to say the words of a prayer without any real involvement in the act of praying. We go through the motions, moving our lips, repeating old phrases, just in case it might make a difference. Or because it gives us a few minutes rest. Or because we don't know what else to do. Sometimes our prayers are more faithful and we are more deeply connected with the Holy if we visualize the people or the situations we are praying for.

May those who sow in tears...

I see a young girl sitting in a doctor's office, where she has come to talk to the doctor. Eighteen months before, her sister cheerfully explained to the doctor that her bottom bled because Daddy had hurt her. The girl I see now, talking to the doctor, says everything at home is fine. Mummy and Daddy are lovely. She doesn't know why her bottom used to bleed.

I see the doctor working and waiting for 18 months, building a relationship of trust with the girl. Lately, the youngster has begun to cry more when she sees the doctor. Now I see her with her head on the doctor's lap, crying and crying, soaking the doctor's skirt with her tears. Yes, she says, someone did hurt her, but she won't tell who. Not unless she can write it down on a piece of paper so the doctor can tear it up after she's read it. Agreed. She writes, Daddy. The doctor reads it, and tears it up. The girl cries harder than ever. Afterwards, when the doctor is alone, the doctor cries too. Their work is going well, but it is not over yet.

May those who sow in tears...

I see a small room, upstairs in a house. Nine women have gathered here, as they have once a week for the last six months; they only see each other in this place for these three hours each week. One thing brings them together – they all had to cope with being sexually abused as children. Initially they came together for support, but over the months they have found friendship, caring, solidarity, hope, and healing. Together they have created a secure place to be in touch with the aftermath of abuse.

I see the women standing in a circle, their arms around each other's waists, huddled close together. Their heads are bowed as if in prayer. No one is talking; all are waiting for someone to begin. When she does, I hear crying, not words. I see tears flowing and her shoulders shaking. The women all hold each other a little tighter. Another starts to cry, louder, grief exploding in short bursts from her throat, and then another, higher-pitched, the sound of terror, and another and another, until all are weeping, wailing, crying out. Streams of tears wash down their faces, while rivers of mucus lengthen and quiver. One by one heads are raised shamelessly as if to petition the walls of the room, the world beyond the room, wherever help might be embodied, wherever the Holy might be found.

May those who sow in tears...

I see a man in his late sixties in his living room with his wife. He has been depressed, and until now refused to talk to anyone about the possible reasons. On good days he makes it through to the afternoon before the weeping starts. On bad days his eyes well up with tears in the morning before he's even out of bed. He is ashamed of himself, ashamed of his crying, and ashamed of the reason why.

Until he retired last year he had a purpose in life. It was important to get up and dressed, go to work, be cheerful, act as though nothing was wrong. He'd practiced that way of being ever since he was seven years old and it first happened.

The woman asks, "What happened?"

Haltingly he describes how his uncle came to live with his family, how at night he'd come into his room and slide into bed with him. The uncle made the boy touch him, touch his private parts, but then it got worse. He made him suck his penis until his mouth filled up with semen, and he'd gag and want to throw up, but more than anything he wanted the uncle to go away. "Don't tell anyone about our secret," warned the uncle. "I'll kill myself if you do."

When the man is finished telling what happened, the woman, his wife, takes his hands in her own, and together they both weep.

◇◇◇◇◇

May those who sow in tears...

Holy One,
    do you see your people weeping,
    and know the reason why?
Do you turn your face towards our grief,
    and share in our sadness?
Are you ashamed, like us, of what has happened?
Do you rage at the injustice and scream in terror?
Do you hurt?
Do you care?
Do you weep?

Holy One,
    some days it is hard to have faith,
    to believe you can do anything to help.
We long for you to kiss the hurt better,
    to dry our eyes and make us well.
Yet our emptiness remains.
There is no quick fix.

Holy One, hear us.
Bring back the days when all was well,
    before we were hurt,
    before we were twelve, or seven, or three, or born.
Fill our emptiness with the trust we used to know.
Let us wake up laughing.
Make us sing all day and night.

◇◇◇◇◇

May those who sow in tears reap with shouts of joy.

Between sowing and reaping there is a time of waiting, a time of faith
and hope. In the intervals between our weeping we are able to rest, breathe
a little more easily, and move more calmly through our days. As we take a
break from the hard work of healing, we begin to imagine life when our
tears are finally over. In the waiting time we are not alone.

Holy One, in the emptiness we know this:
    there is no going back,
    and no miraculous cure,
only your presence with us,
    for us, not against us.
In the emptiness we hear you,
    weeping over us,
    working to bring about justice and new life.
In the quiet of our rest
    you cradle us tenderly,
    washing our faces with tears from your own.

Then, O Holy One,
    when your tears too are dry,
    we hear instead of weeping, a distant tune.
Unfamiliar, it calls us to listen.
We see on your face a knowing smile of recognition
    and as the music approaches, spreading glee.
Then you join the melody,
    you become the music and it becomes you.

You are singing now, not weeping,
   and more than that,
you are dancing,
   only more than that,
you are full of joy,
   you are joy,
and you cradle us still.

Singing, dancing, cradling joy:
As the music subsides it is your turn to rest.
Ever so carefully, you set us down,
   refreshed and blessed for our journey on.
A quantum leap ahead of when you first found us,
   emptiness welcomes us,
   promising life in all abundance.
We are certain now, as never before,
   we are on our way home,
   we shall shout out with joy.

◇◇◇◇◇

Questions to ask ourselves

- What gradual growth and change for the better can I see in my life? Am I impatient with the slowness of transformation?
- How do I understand healing to be work?
- When do I weep? Who weeps with me?
- What do I "see" when I pray "May those who sow in tears…"?
- Can I cultivate periods of respite to intersperse amongst my work?
- What do I "see" when I imagine "reaping with shouts of joy"?

Will you have a little hold?

In the time of King Herod, after Jesus was born in Bethlehem of Judea, wise men from the East came to Jerusalem, asking, "Where is the child who has been born king of the Jews? For we observed his star at its rising, and have come to pay him homage." When King Herod heard this, he was frightened, and all Jerusalem with him; and calling together all the chief priests and scribes of the people, he inquired of them where the Messiah was to be born. They told him, "In Bethlehem of Judea; for so it has been written by the prophet:

'And you, Bethlehem, in the land of Judah,

are by no means least among the rulers of Judah;

for from you shall come a ruler

who is to shepherd my people Israel.'"

Then Herod secretly called for the wise men and learned from them the exact time when the star had appeared. Then he sent them to Bethlehem, saying, "Go and search diligently for the child; and when you have found him, bring me word so that I may also go and pay him homage." When they had heard the king, they set out; and there, ahead of them, went the star that they had seen at its rising, until it stopped over the place where the child was. When they saw that the star had stopped, they were overwhelmed with joy. On entering the house, they saw the child with Mary his mother; and they knelt down and paid him homage. Then, opening their treasure chests, they offered him gifts of gold, frankincense, and myrrh. And having been warned in a dream not to return to Herod, they left for their own country by another road.

MATTHEW 2:1-12

The priest at the Anglican church I attended in North Wales one Epiphany Sunday began his sermon by recounting a visit to friends who had a newborn baby. It was several years before he had children of his own and before he had any experience with babies, so when his friends asked him, "Will you have a little hold?" he was filled with fear and trepidation.

As I sat there, I remembered being in a similar situation myself when I was only 19. The parents with the new baby were friends of friends, and I didn't have any particular interest in the newborn child. At least not until I saw him. To my surprise I found myself oohing and aahing along with everyone else at his perfect features, tiny hands and even tinier fingers, and his apparent total contentment with life. My friends held and cuddled the child for a while, before passing him back to his mother. Then she turned to me and said, "Will you have a little hold, too?"

Suddenly the wonder that had given rise to my oohing and aahing evaporated and I was filled with terror. How could I take into my arms such a perfect little being? I didn't know how to hold anything so tiny and so vulnerable. I was terrified I might accidentally hurt him, out of ignorance and clumsiness. Before I could formulate a decent way of saying, "Don't be offended, but no, that's all right thank you," the baby was held out to me. I had no choice except to close my hands around his small frame, and support the weight of his little body. As I sat cradling him in my arms my terror never went away, but I also felt amazement, tenderness, wonder, and joy. For the few minutes that I held him, I was oblivious to everything and everyone else in the room; there was just his warmth resting on me, the softness of his skin, the shine in his wispy hair, the wrinkles around the knuckles of his fingers.

When my attention returned to the church service, I heard the priest say that Christmas is a time when our Creator asks us, "Will you have a little hold?" – not only in our imaginations of the baby Jesus, not only of newborn babies in general, but of anyone who shares in their vulnerability, their need, and their utter reliance on others for food, shelter, comfort, or warmth. Will we have a little hold of anyone who is blatantly dependent on others for caring, love, respect, and a continuation of life? He named some of the vulnerable groups in society: the unemployed, terminally ill cancer patients, refugees fleeing violence...

My own list of vulnerable people includes everybody who has had to endure childhood sexual abuse. I think of an older man who heard me read some of my poetry, who told me afterwards he too had been abused. When he gave me a hug, he crumpled tearfully in my arms. I didn't know what to do or say, so I just held him until he regained his composure. Then a gentle smile spread across his wrinkled face and he said, "Isn't it wonderful we can talk about it at last, after a lifetime of keeping it a secret?" I was amazed all over again at the resiliency some people have.

I think of a five-year-old child I knew, years ago. I suspected she was being sexually abused. It was before the days that the police or social services responded to a report based only on reasonable suspicion, and I never told anybody who could have intervened. She was a spunky little girl, overflowing with energy, curiosity, sensitivity, and humor. I did what I could to affirm her as often as possible. She is a young adult now; I hope she's okay.

I think of a woman in her thirties who has accused her mother, a friend of mine, of sexually abusing her when she was a small child. Although I know nobody is exempt from being an abuser, in this case it just doesn't ring true. What seems possible is that someone else was responsible, but the daughter is too afraid to name the actual abuser, even to herself. Perhaps blaming her mother feels slightly more "safe" than blaming the one who is really guilty. How does my friend continue to care for and love her daughter? How do I care for my friend, except by listening to her talk about the child she has all but lost? Occasionally she shares some of her anger and grief. Amazingly, she also talks fondly about her daughter, and treasures the good times they used to have together.

Do those of us who were violated in infancy dare to imagine what it would be like to hold in our arms the baby we once were? If we do, we discover how helpless we were. We know the impossibility of doing anything to stop the terrible things that happened. We discover we didn't do a thing to deserve being hurt. None of it was our fault. All babies are innocent – you, me, Jesus…

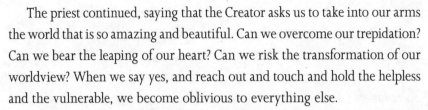

The priest continued, saying that the Creator asks us to take into our arms the world that is so amazing and beautiful. Can we overcome our trepidation? Can we bear the leaping of our heart? Can we risk the transformation of our worldview? When we say yes, and reach out and touch and hold the helpless and the vulnerable, we become oblivious to everything else.

He makes it sound so easy, but I have found that saying unequivocally "Yes, I will treasure the world my Creator is asking me to hold" is difficult to do. The earliest relationships in my life did not treasure me, did not value my delight with life. Can I ever regain the spontaneity and trust that I lost?

Around the time I first began to remember having been abused, my own children were four and two. Thankfully, they were usually content and easy to be with, and other adults generally commented on how delightful they were. Most of the time I was able to compartmentalize looking after them and coping with the raw pain of memories. But sometimes I could hardly bear to be with them.

When I saw them asleep in their beds at night their vulnerability was a painful reminder of how my own vulnerability had been exploited. I wanted so badly to keep them safe, at the same time as fostering their curiosity, independence, and spirit of adventure. Yes, my heart often leapt with fear that something would come along and snuff out all the delight that life held for them.

When their playing together turned into squabbling, I thought I would explode with rage. In my own childhood, fights with my siblings were cited as a cause for my father abusing me, and I was furious when my children exposed me to that risk again. Of course, I knew that in reality my father was thousands of miles away, and there was no risk. But knowing how irrational my reaction was did nothing to soften it.

The transformation of my worldview means a transformation of the horrible experiences of my past. Not that what happened can ever be undone. But knowing how hard it is to say "Yes" even to my small world as a mother,

I renew my commitment to healing, whatever form and however long it takes.

I rejoined the sermon to hear that the event we call Epiphany was not a sudden revelation, but a gradual process. The journey for the wise travelers was long; the star led them for many months, not just for one night. The revelation that the Creator is incarnate, embodied, present in the very stuff of our world, takes a lifetime to appreciate fully.

It is more comfortable to believe in the Christmas story as it applies to other people. I can accept the embodiment of the Divine in the very young and the very old, in the homeless and the chronically sick, and even in drug addicts and sex trade workers. But the notion that incarnation has anything to do with me personally is puzzling. Splitting off from my body was the mechanism I used to cope with the physical pain of abuse. I found consolation with a divine presence out of my body, not in my body. I have had to learn how to reconnect with and be aware of myself in my body and with its sensations, and have yet to learn how to do this consistently and without making a conscious effort.

The birth of Jesus was a grand extravaganza by the Artist of the Universe insistent on getting attention: hence the angels cavorting with shepherds in the middle of the night; hence the star calling the wisest of the wise to visit a little child; hence the holy leap of faith in expecting Mary and Joseph to do their part. It is similarly a leap of faith for adults who were sexually abused as children to move from fear, and from isolation even from ourselves, to trust and connection with the meaning of Christmas. Can the cultivation of wonder help? Can the practice of mindfulness keep us grounded in the here and now, so that we "see," with all of who we are, the tender, beautiful, awesome moments that intersect our lives each day?

The priest told us that a daily practice of being aware of the Holy in the poor and the needy of the world, and reaching out in love, is required if the Christmas story is to be more than mere sentimentality. Remember the commitment of the three travelers. Remember Mary and Joseph who never broke the trust that had been placed in them to protect and nurture the holy child Jesus.

Jesus was blessed to have parents who looked after him in the way all children need looking after. Most parents find it hard to be consistently patient, kind, trusting, and self-confident in the way Mary and Joseph are traditionally portrayed. It's an even greater challenge for us if our childhood involved the secret of sexual abuse eroding our confidence in both ourselves and the world at large.

As the priest says, it is a daily practice to reach out in love. It means being intentional and deliberate about how we live each day. The wise travelers committed themselves to a physical journey to visit the holy child. We have to commit to a different journey, a physical, psychological and spiritual journey, to visit the One who is incarnate, vulnerable, present with us, and even within us on earth today. It is a journey that leads us to contemporary Herods as well as to angels who guard and guide; it is a journey through anguish and misery and a journey with good companions; it is a journey with an uncertain destination. And yet it is also a journey with the certainty of wonder along the way.

"Will you have a little hold?" is an invitation from the Holy One to reach out and hold the vulnerable.

But before the sermon ends, another image comes to mind. It is the image of a baby reaching out and instinctively closing her hand around the finger of a grown-up hand, and holding on to her immediate world. We need to learn that too – to live in the moment, to reach out and hold tight to what is firm and strong. When we hear the Holy One extend that invitation to us, we can be sure of an abundance of opportunities to overcome our fear and trepidation, and to say a resounding, "Yes."

◇◇◇◇◇

Questions to ask ourselves

- What is my sense of being treasured as a youngster? Was being vulnerable and helpless safe for me?
- What part of my life is most in need of transformation? Do I want it to happen?
- What do I understand by incarnation? Is incarnation something that stirs up wonder and joy, or fear and trembling?
- Who do I consider to be vulnerable, and what is my responsibility towards them?
- When have I needed, and been offered, something reliable and secure to hold on to?

A conspiracy of love

Six days later, Jesus took with him Peter and James and John, and led them up a high mountain apart, by themselves. And he was transfigured before them, and his clothes became dazzling white, such as no one on earth could bleach them. And there appeared to them Elijah with Moses, who were talking with Jesus. Then Peter said to Jesus, "Rabbi, it is good for us to be here; let us make three dwellings, one for you, one for Moses, and one for Elijah." He did not know what to say, for they were terrified. Then a cloud overshadowed them, and from the cloud there came a voice, "This is my Son, the Beloved; listen to him!" Suddenly when they looked around, they saw no one with them anymore, but only Jesus. As they were coming down the mountain, he ordered them to tell no one about what they had seen, until after the Son of Man had risen from the dead.

MARK 9:2-9

Usually read in churches on the last Sunday of the Epiphany season, this text tells of a transforming event in Jesus' life when he emanated a brilliant radiance on a mountain in the presence of three of his disciples. Traditionally this is understood to be a revelation of divine glory shining through the person of Jesus. The simultaneous appearance of Moses and Elijah, who were both long dead, is a sign that Jesus' ministry supports the sacred teachings of the law and the prophets. The voice speaking from within a cloud is a sign of the Holy One reiterating the blessing that was given at Jesus' baptism.

Taken alone, this event known as the Transfiguration inspires the reader with wonder and awe, even though we might suspect its full meaning is hidden from us. The context in which it occurs is equally significant. The event happens six days after Jesus' first prediction of his suffering and death, and immediately before Jesus begins his journey to Jerusalem where the prediction is fulfilled with his execution. Superficially, the glorious appearance of Jesus on the mountain in between times marked by trouble and misunderstanding seems out of place. However, at a deeper level the Transfiguration speaks of the enduring purpose and presence of the Creator in the midst of human struggles and suffering. Jesus' commitment to follow his own teachings about justice and truth are matched by a holy commitment from the Source of Life and Love.

At the time the disciples who witnessed Jesus' sudden radiant appearance were confused about what was going on. They found it terrifying, and yet Peter's offer to make individual dwellings for Moses, Elijah, and Jesus suggests he wanted to capture the moment and find a way to make it last. Later on, after they have come down from the mountain and Jesus again predicts his suffering and death, the disciples still don't understand; they seem not to make any connection with the revelation on the mountain. Not until the Resurrection do they fully comprehend.

We might well ask what connection could there possibly be between Jesus' glorious transformation on a mountaintop and child sexual abuse. What place is there for wonder and awe in the exploitation of a youngster? What signs are there of the presence of the Divine in the terrible aftermath and the long struggle to heal? Surely in a situation full of pain and terror, bleak desperation is more likely than shining radiance.

Yet those who suffer sexual abuse and its consequences do occasionally experience a glorious reality that intercepts their agony and confusion. By grace it can sustain us on our journey through the horrors and on towards eventual resurrected living.

◇◇◇◇◇

It is wintertime. I have been visiting for a few days in my home town in the North of England. Ever since I arrived it has been snowing, but on my last day here I wake up to clear skies and decide to go for a walk on the North Yorkshire moors. I have spent the last few days reconnecting with people from my past to see if they can help me make sense of what happened when I was young. It will be good to have some time alone.

I set off up an incline that follows the path of a disused railway line, climbing steadily from the valley up onto the high open moors. There is snow everywhere, reshaping the landscape; it is mounded over gorse bushes and clumps of heather, it is blown into cornices at the scarp edge of the moor, and it fashions the rocks with their hard edges into soft pillows. Scraggly windswept trees have been transformed into fascinating sculptures. After an hour or so of climbing, I am on top of the moors, gazing at mile after mile of snow, my path a smooth ribbon bisecting undulating fields of white.

There are some who don't appreciate the beauty of moorland. They are bored by what they see as flat sameness, generally dark and threatening. But on a day like this even they could not deny the breathtaking beauty. They would see in the blanket of snow a welcome disguise, concealing the usual ugly bleakness. But they would be wrong. A transfiguration has taken place that reveals more of the beauty that is present even without the snow. I have loved the moors all my life, and found a freedom here in every season of the year and in every kind of weather. What I see today is their usual beauty magnified a hundredfold.

I walk most of the afternoon, thankful to be alone, thankful for this place and all its brilliance and peace. I wish I knew how to make this time last. I am all too aware that my most profound experiences of well-being, or connectedness, or love, are chunked into separate entities, like intricate and perfect crystals, distinct from all else. Although these moments are real enough, I can never convey them properly, never bring them to bear fully on the struggles that make up so much of my life. A few of them come to mind as I walk across the moors.

I think of my brother and the summer he and I shared a new hobby; we spent several weeks digging fossils out of coastal shale together. I had just written school exams to determine whether or not I would go on to university. Everybody else was sure that I would have done well, but waiting for the results that summer was an anxious time for me. It seemed to be a matter of survival that I leave home as soon as possible, and going away to university was a sure way of that happening. As my brother and I chiseled away at the rocks I hoped for the best and planned for the worst. If my fears came true and I had failed abysmally, then I would find a clerical job and save up enough money until I could afford to move out of my parents' home. I never talked about this to my brother or to anyone, but his easy presence beside me day after day was a great comfort.

I think of the time my oldest sister asked for my help with her work. Being four years older than me, she was usually the one to help me, so I was glad of an opportunity to reciprocate. She was an English teacher and wanted me to play classical guitar music to accompany her and her students as they recited The Four Quartets by T. S. Eliot. I wasn't especially good on the guitar, but I enjoyed playing, and I was honored that she had asked me.

I remember the lifting of one particular bout of depression during my undergraduate years. I was walking across the lawn at college, the grass still glistening with dew, and the early morning sun splashing color on the trees. I had only recently become a Christian, and knew nothing about angels, but it seemed to me that a throng of heavenly beings was singing loud Alleluias in the air all around.

I remember going to visit friends from seminary a few days after I first recalled incidents of sexual abuse. When I arrived they could easily see that I was distressed. They invited me in, and made tea while I sought the words to tell them my trouble. It was impossible though. All I could say was, "It's too difficult to talk about right now." I suppose I expected them to push me a little, to ask leading questions, and if that didn't work then to try to cheer me up. Instead, they simply said, "That's okay; you don't need to talk. We're just happy you're here with us; you don't have to be alone." Their words were a miracle of grace breaking through the barrier of isolation and despair.

I remember meeting with two friends the evening before I went to talk to the Bishop about being abused in a church in his diocese. We were intensely focused on the task at hand – rehearsing what I needed to say, making sure I could take care of myself through the conversation, and being realistic about the possible outcomes. My friends were as determined as I was that what I had to say would not go unsaid, whether because of my fear or because of the Church's unwillingness to hear it. Their solidarity and compassion were a blessing to me, giving me courage to face whatever might happen the next day.

By the time I turn around to walk home, the sun is low in the sky. I will have to hurry to be home before dark. In one final gesture of gratitude I scoop up a handful of loose snow and throw it high into the air, so that small clumps and flakes shower down on me. I recall that every single snowflake has a different crystal structure. Suddenly there is before me a vision of the crystals that in my mind contain love. Shining brightly they dance in the sky; each one is unique, but their movements are synchronized. I am dazzled by the conspiracy of love that has been at work throughout my life, guiding me towards awareness and truth, pointing me in the direction of home. Right in front of my eyes, angels and friends, my sisters and brother, music and poetry, moors and trees, grass and rocks are transformed into glory, assuring me that the mystery of holiness will always be with me.

By the time the snow I tossed into the air has all fallen back to earth, the sky is streaked with gold and joy is spread across my face. I have given up my resistance, and given in to Love.

◇◇◇◇◇

O Holy Brilliance,
    the beginning and the end of wonder,
    you surprise me, dazzle me,
take my breath away.

When I am far from your glory
    you come and scoop me up.
You hold me close to your shining face;
you breathe strength into my being.

Then, satisfied that I believe in your goodness,
    you gently set me down again.
Your fire lives in my soul.
Your love burns in my heart.
Your passion transforms my deepest yearnings
    into joy.

◇◇◇◇◇

Questions to ask ourselves

- What crystals of wonder do I recall from my childhood? My adolescence? My adult life?
- At critical times of my healing, who has been there for me? How have they given relief?
- What images does the word "glory" evoke for me?
- Do I have a connection with nature that sustains me through difficult times?
- Do I welcome solitude in my life? Am I afraid of solitude?

Part 4

Grace

Beyond betrayal

Now the betrayer had given them a sign, saying, "The one I will kiss is the man;
arrest him and lead him away under guard." So when Jesus came, Judas went
up to him at once and said, "Rabbi!" and kissed him. Then they laid hands on
Jesus and arrested him.

MARK 14:44-46

Judas first appears in the gospel of Mark as one of the twelve that Jesus appoints
to accompany him in his ministry of proclamation and healing, although even
in his introduction Judas is identified as the one who betrayed Jesus. Whatever
else Judas did as a follower of Jesus, the gospel writer remembers him mainly
for his betrayal. According to Mark, Jesus himself knows that Judas will turn
against him, and warns that the consequences for the betrayer will be even
worse than the consequences for the betrayed. When Jesus does nothing to
prevent Judas carrying out his plan to give him away to the authorities, it is
presumably because he realizes that ultimately there is nothing he can do.

Judas' betrayal of Jesus is all the more shocking because of the way it happens. Clearly Judas was very close to Jesus, and knew as much about him as
any of the disciples. He played the part of loyal follower and friend throughout
Jesus' ministry, and it was natural that he would eat and drink the Passover
meal with Jesus; Judas' final kiss was a telling gesture of intimacy.

Any questions the reader might have about Judas' motives go unanswered.
We might wonder whether he was afraid of the implications of Jesus' radical
preaching, or whether perhaps he was greedy for the money the authorities
promised him. When we focus too much attention on Judas we risk being
distracted from what Jesus endured because of him. However, it is hard to
give up wanting answers to the question, "Why?" It is hard to accept the
notion that nothing could have prevented his betrayal.

Whenever a child is sexually exploited, betrayal abounds. At the very least
there is betrayal of a child's physical and emotional vulnerability, and his/her
natural tendency to trust. If the child knows the person responsible, then the

sense of betrayal is accentuated by former experiences of that person behaving kindly and fairly. Non-abusers who know, or ought to know, when a child is being hurt and do nothing to stop it, are also guilty of betrayal.

Children are betrayed by grownups who tuck them into bed at night and read them a bedtime story, only to return later to have their sexual desires met. Children are betrayed by teachers and family friends who see signs of abuse yet who do and say nothing. Children are betrayed by silence or laughter or normal conversation at breakfast in the morning, just a few hours after they have been violated. Children are betrayed by a society that expects them to keep themselves safe, and yet does not do enough to make their world intrinsically safe.

After the abuse is over and we are ready to begin the healing process, all too often we encounter fresh betrayal. Counselors whom we thought we could trust minimize the impact of what we suffered. Church ministers are impatient with us for our reluctance to forgive. Family members to whom we disclose stop inviting us to the usual family gatherings, as though we were the ones who had done something wrong. Friends tell us to get over it, we have said enough already. Government-run healthcare systems lack imagination, understanding, and resources to be of much help. Courts of law offer more protection to offenders than justice to complainants.

Those of us who have been betrayed live with the ambiguity of having received friendship and even love from the same person who becomes our enemy. What, if anything, does our faith have to say? What comfort is there in Jesus' prophecy of woe to betrayers, when what we most want is for our betrayers to turn their backs on their treachery and apologize to us for the harm they allowed? We want them still to honor our trust, our vulnerability, and our irrational desire for a loving relationship with them.

◇◇◇◇◇

Remembering a story in *Poppies on the Rubbish Heap* by Madge Bray, I see a little girl taken from the care of her birth parents because their care was no-care, their cuddles were sexualized, and the best they did for her was to abandon her to her own resources. I see her in a foster home; a nice young couple who couldn't have their own children are looking for a perfect girl-child to complement the older boy they recently adopted. She will make them into a normal nuclear family.

I see her sitting on her new daddy's lap, her hands going straight for his crotch. He slaps her, pushes her off, and calls on the new mummy to get her away from him. The new mummy is shocked and tells her new daughter Daddy won't love her if she ever does that again. The girl is confused. She was just doing what she had been taught. Puzzled she asks, "You want, I shag your face?" The woman blushes, can't believe her ears, calls the social work authorities and asks that they come and take the child away. She's not what they wanted; not the nice, polite child they need to show off to the relatives in the same way they might show off a fancy new car.

The little girl, betrayed by her first family, betrayed by the authorities who delivered her to this foster family, is now betrayed a third time by their small-minded and selfish expectations. Fortunately her next foster parents use their down-to-earth wisdom and common sense; healing begins to happen for the little girl, and eventually she is adopted by another family who love her and delight in her. A kind of resurrection takes place, yet the question remains. Why the betrayals?

◇◇◇◇◇

I listen to church leaders describe their work of justice-making with Canadian First Nations people. I see a man who, like so many of his generation, was taken away from his village and placed in a government sponsored, church run residential school in a city hundreds of kilometers away. Sexual abuse was just one of the many atrocities this man endured at the school. Now as an adult he and other men and women have spoken out about the betrayal of trust they suffered as children. An alternative resolution process has brought public and personal apologies from the church, and also financial compensation.

But there is still some measure of betrayal, for what this man would like more than anything is a continuing relationship with those who heard him share his story, his agony and pain. But, when the hearings are over, everyone goes back to their own homes, and they will likely never see each other again.

Furthermore there is continuing betrayal within the institution. The widespread relief that the church has not gone bankrupt in the process of settling claims betrays the seriousness of the harm done to former students of residential schools. The overriding desire on the part of most church members – for light at the end of the tunnel and a time when they won't have to talk about this anymore – is a betrayal of the trust of all those who have brought the truth before the church. Like Judas they cannot bear the cost of holding fast to truth. They cannot face the loss of innocence that comes with admitting their faith community is guilty of having created an environment in which children were not safe. They refuse to grasp that the journey for those abused in residential schools will last their entire life, and that the church's journey – if it is to be of any lasting value – must be at least as long.

◇◇◇◇◇

In my own childhood, my mother was my primary caregiver. In some ways she was also the one who betrayed me the most. I have found it as hard to heal what she did and did not do as to heal what my abusers did. My efforts to force myself to move beyond feeling bitter and vengeful were always thwarted. Over the years indignation and rage towards my mother became confused with frustration for not finding a way to let go. As with so much of the healing process I had to wait for an internal shifting to happen spontaneously.

When I read carefully the account of Judas' betrayal of Jesus I am surprised and even offended by Jesus' acceptance of what Judas does. I want to shake Jesus by the shoulders and tell him not to be so passive, but to reprimand Judas for being such a rotten friend and trickster. I want to avoid reading any further, because I know what happens next. Jesus lets go of any disappointment, or anger, or bitterness towards Judas and goes forward to his death.

Am I afraid that if I let go of my strong feelings towards my mother that I will have to die? Or am I unwilling to admit deep down the connection between her betrayal and the terrible abuse that followed? Staying with my discomfort of Jesus' letting go of Judas led me eventually to write the following. I had gone away alone on a silent retreat ostensibly for a time of renewal, but in reality out of desperation to "deal with my mother's betrayal" once and for all.

◇◇◇◇◇

Lately I have been obsessing about my mother's betrayal more than usual, but I have managed very well not to deal with it. Nothing whatsoever has shifted. I find myself rehearsing a well-worn litany of the bad she did and the good she failed to do, as though I'm in the confessional, recounting her sins and asking for penance and absolution on her behalf. No. That's not true. I have no desire for her to be forgiven. I am not her priestly intermediary to heaven, but rather her prosecutor, bound and determined to ensure that not an iota of her wrongdoing is ever let go. I could spend the rest of my life cast in this role and never be free. The only miniscule sign that I have made any progress is that I am becoming ever so slightly bored by my repetitions of her crimes.

At the retreat house there is a labyrinth in the garden; I stumble upon it by accident on my way home after a vigorous walk, pounding the pavement. I had been trying to get rid of my mother by stamping her into the ground. Before I go back to my room I decide to walk the labyrinth. Perhaps it will calm me down.

I put my knapsack on a nearby bench and walk to the entrance. Then I walk back to the bench, take off my shoes, and return barefoot to the wide green opening, bordered on left and right by sun-bleached bricks. Suddenly I am nervous. I had best get this over with. I will spiral in and out quickly and then go indoors for a cup of tea.

But my legs and feet will hardly move. I am pulled back into myself where I feel the warmth of soft grass on the soles of my feet. Focusing on the ground just in front of me I see the "grass" is mostly moss and small flowers, yellow ones I can't identify, and white clover. A few insects are grazing on the path. I pay attention to make sure there are no bees. I remember my mother telling the story of how I once almost stood on a bee and it flew up and stung me on my ear. Then I think of my sister and her phobia of stinging insects. I used to get impatient with her over it, until she told me they used to tie her up to a plum tree heavy with overripe fruit and buzzing with wasps. Rage rises in me; I am not the only one my mother betrayed.

I draw my awareness back to my feet, and feel again the ground beneath them. It is not so warm now. The path has brought me to a place in the labyrinth that is shaded by a large tree. I walk very slowly, and go to a place deep within that is too often frozen in time and space. Here I feel the raw fear that accompanies betrayal, as fresh as the first time I encountered it. I know the burden of its powerlessness, a weight pressing hard within me. I struggle to stay with it, breathing through the emotions, breathing in pain, breathing out a desire for relief. This time, in this place, I don't disassociate. I stay put, gasping in short breaths of air, breathing out more slowly, a process not unlike managing the pain of childbirth. I sense that here and now I am giving birth to a new way of being. Staying put, facing fear, moving beyond betrayal.

I continue walking, each footstep carefully placed. I feel the taut energy that accompanies thoughts of my mother move through my body, down my legs and out through my feet into the ground. I am aware of letting go; aware of the paradox of letting go as a deliberate act over which I have no control. Like the tears rolling down my face.

The path leads me out of the shade to where the grass is warm again. I remember walking barefoot on sand dunes in summertime near a small fishing village our mother used to take us to for holidays. I smile; tears run over my lips and into my mouth; salty water, like the sea. Mum was not all bad. I have some good memories.

The turns on the path get tighter as I come closer to the center. I swing around one bend and my eyes trip over a single purple flower. I laugh a thank you as I go by, thinking of Alice Walker and friends who would be glad to know that I didn't "piss It off" by not noticing. It – the Holy Other – is all around: in the sweet smell of clover and the velvet of moss; in the coolness underfoot again; in the song of the swallows and the silence of my walking. I waltz a large circle in the labyrinth's heart before setting outwards.

I want to make the journey out last as long as possible even though, when I lift my eyes to the maples and cedars surrounding this place of transformation, the trees tell me they – and the world – will welcome me. I take the turns wide so as to extend the walk. The alternating shade and light, coolness and warmth are very good. The purple surprises me all over again; I greet it in return. Jealous clover sends out extra fragrance and thanksgiving spreads across my face. I pay attention to the dry leaves, fallen and scattered on the ground, aware that I have been avoiding stepping on them. They remind me of the countless betrayals I have known that have lost their life now. They are mulch for the earth and for my soul, already becoming food for new growth.

Letting go of the hard emotions associated with betrayal creates an emptiness within me. Not an emptiness of grief and sadness, but rather of waiting and anticipation. There is commitment here, too; a steady knowing that although I let go of reciting the litany of wrongdoing, and of nursing hurt feelings, I am not saying what happened doesn't matter anymore. There is a freedom about the emptiness that makes it possible for me to speak, to act, to listen and pray in ways that are more likely to address continuing betrayal of others. Here and there the grass of the labyrinth spreads over the curving bricks. If it weren't for someone caring for the path all the bricks would be invisible. If it weren't for many people caring for little ones who have been hurt, the path towards a future free from abuse would be very difficult to find.

Only a half circle remains between me and the opening to the world beyond this holy place. I return to the soles of my feet, through which healing has happened, and take the last few steps towards a new freedom.

Thank you to the earth and to my feet.
Thank you to the sun that warms the ground,
    and the trees that shade it.
Thank you to the purple and the yellow,
    and the clover of course,
    and to the green grass and mosses.
Thank you to the wholly present Holy Other
    who transforms and recreates,
    who invites us into her heart
    and sends us out to her world.

◇◇◇◇◇

Questions to ask ourselves

- How have I been betrayed as a child? As an adult? How did I feel and what were the consequences?
- Do I ever feel as though the Creator has betrayed me – for example, by not intervening to protect me?
- How do I feel now towards people who have betrayed me?
- Can I articulate what purpose holding on to past betrayals might serve?
- When I think of Judas' betrayal of Jesus, what would I like to say to Judas? – and to Jesus?
- What would I like to say to those people who have betrayed me?

Holy work

When it was evening on that day, the first day of the week, and the doors of the
house where the disciples had met were locked for fear of the Jews, Jesus came
and stood among them and said, "Peace be with you." After he said this, he
showed them his hands and his side. Then the disciples rejoiced when they saw
the Lord. Jesus said to them again, "Peace be with you. As the Father has sent
me, so I send you." When he had said this, he breathed on them and said to
them, "Receive the Holy Spirit. If you forgive the sins of any, they are forgiven
them; if you retain the sins of any, they are retained."

JOHN 20:19-23

◇◇◇◇◇

O Great Creator:
just today
I would like your word to be black and white,
and if that cannot be
then black or white,
for I have known too much of
blotchy gray mottled ambiguity,
absence of certainty,
conversation without conclusion,
unclear directions
to wanderers such as me.

Just this once will you
give not only your word
but also have the last
word?

◇◇◇◇◇

It is hard to argue against the centrality of forgiveness to the main strands of Christian tradition. The Church's teaching can be summarized something like this: Jesus died to forgive our sins, and we in turn must forgive other people. So strong is this message that it often seems to have the qualities of a commandment. In many respects, "You must forgive others" weighs more heavily than, "You must love others."

Then those of us who have suffered greatly because of the wrongdoing of others face the awful choice of either forcing ourselves to forgive or turning away from our faith.

The struggle with forgiveness takes many forms. For some it replaces other struggles necessary for healing, meaning that feelings of fear, rage, injustice, and isolation have to be buried deeper than ever in order to maintain a forgiving front. For others who rush into expressing forgiveness to their abusers, there can be feelings of great confusion when the love they crave is still not given, and the peace they seek remains elusive.

The struggle is seen in many ways.

A middle-aged woman was raped as a teenager by her father. She has recently learned that he also abused her daughter, his granddaughter. Her adult daughter wants to press charges with the police. Through clenched teeth she says to her daughter, "I don't support you in that because I love him and forgive him, and never want to be moved from this position. Leave me alone and let me heal."

A young white Canadian has been learning about Aboriginal spirituality, and has adopted some of its practices for himself. He has participated in ceremonies which involve the symbolic offering of favorite food to his deceased uncle who used to abuse him. But the young man is disappointed and frustrated that he continues to be haunted by what his uncle did.

An elderly woman was a bystander to her children's abuse. She refuses to talk about what happened except to say to her children, "Can't you forgive an old woman her sins?"

There is something unsettled and unsettling in each situation. In the first, there is a glaring contrast between the woman's stated feelings of love and forgiveness towards her abusive father, and her overt hostility to her own daughter who is seeking justice. Why does the woman say she never wants to be moved from her position unless she still feels threatened and on shaky ground? Is it possible for genuine love and sincere forgiveness to be withdrawn? Notice also that she sees her healing as happening after forgiveness. Is it not more natural for the process of healing with its chaos of emotions of rage, dread, fear, and shame to precede forgiveness?

The ceremony in which a nephew offers his abusive uncle his favorite food speaks of great generosity which ought to be a sign of forgiveness. Yet the young man still feels haunted. Could it be that he is somehow hoping to feel forgiveness by performing an act of forgiveness? This would be akin to standing at the finish line of a marathon hoping to invoke the feeling of great achievement that only comes with actually running the course.

The person who asks in her old age for forgiveness without any willingness to converse with those she has wronged, and without much indication of sadness or regret – not to mention repentance – can manipulate others into feeling guilty, ashamed, and mean-spirited. It can be tempting to say out of frustration and hopelessness, "All right, I forgive you. Now, maybe what you did and what you failed to do to protect me won't bother me anymore." But true forgiveness is not given reluctantly. Rather it is a generous, selfless, costly, and grace-filled act.

◇◇◇◇◇

Careful consideration of the passage from John 20 helps to elaborate the complex issue of forgiveness. Jesus risen from the dead greets the disciples with, "Peace be with you," and passes on to them the mission that he had from God. Then he breathes into them the Holy Spirit, which empowers them to forgive and to retain sins. A comparison with Matthew 18:18 reinforces Jesus' teaching that whatever the disciples forgive is also forgiven in heaven, and that whatever the disciples retain is also retained in heaven. This implies that the act of forgiving or not forgiving reaches beyond this world to the heavenly realm. Choosing to forgive – or not – is holy work. There is no indication that either choice is better than the other. The decision is left to the disciples, and to all people of faith who have received the Holy Spirit.

This is amazing good news to people who cannot in all honesty forgive those who have wronged them. It presents a serious challenge to the weight of traditional dogma that demands we must always forgive. It means we are not excluded from the promises of faith simply on the basis of choosing not to forgive.

The internal and external voices telling those who have been sexually abused that they must forgive still need to be taken seriously, lest we underestimate their power. Not only the Church in its teachings, hymns, and prayers is culpable, but so are non-offending family members who make excuses for abusers: "Your grandfather is under a lot of stress right now; try to understand him and forgive him." Even some abusers themselves ask forgiveness from their young victims: "I only do this because I love you, and sometimes love has to hurt just a little bit. Can you forgive me, sweetie? Here, let's dry your eyes and see you smile."

Children surrounded by expectations to forgive quickly internalize the message. They need so strongly to believe that the grownups in their lives love them that they make sense of the abuse by thinking that they must have done something wrong to deserve it. Another coping strategy is to split off from the pain and confusion, and so manage to get on with everyday life by denying that anything bad ever happened.

Healing and truth-telling necessarily mean an end to denial, and an end to self-blaming. At any given stage, they also involve a conscious decision not to forgive or to forgive. Not forgiving means that there is still some kind of connection, some holding to account, some setting of firm boundaries with the abuser, all of which are important and of holy significance. Not forgiving does not mean seeking revenge, even though that might be what we feel we want. The best "revenge" is to live another day and to heal, and otherwise leave revenge to the Creator.

For the woman who says she forgives her father's abuse, and just wants to be left alone to heal, a healthier response to her daughter would be: "I am very, very sorry that he abused you too. I thought I had forgiven him, but when I learn that he abused you the feelings of rage and terror are stronger than ever. For myself I don't want to press charges at this time, and yet I would like to honor your decision to do that. Can we work together to find a way through this difficult time so that what he did to us doesn't divide us and doesn't control us any longer?"

The young man who wants to be free from the painful memories of being hurt by his uncle needs permission and support to feel and work through the range of emotions buried deep inside. He could benefit from telling more about what took place, and listening to others share the impact of abuse on them. It is unrealistic to think that he will be truly free from his past until he has faced it in all its ugliness.

The woman who was a bystander to her children's abuse could have said: "If only I had been less preoccupied with keeping out of harm's way myself I would have realized and done something to stop it. I can hardly bear to hear you tell me all that happened. I am ripped apart by anger at what happened to you and guilt that I let it happen. I messed up then, and I don't want to mess up now."

◇◇◇◇◇

Holy One
I have gathered my courage together
    to stand steady in this place,
    this clearing in the forest above the sea
    overlooking the low islands in the East
    silhouetted against the evening sky.
With my feet planted firmly on the ground
    my eyes are searching, scavenging the present beauty
    for a sure sign of your company.
All my senses are alert to the time of your arrival.

(I once thought I could not be this bold
    until I was perfectly ready to receive you;
foolish in retrospect, since only in receiving you
    is perfection even remotely possible.)

The faintest breeze blows through the hawthorn trees.
The open sky almost imperceptibly darkens.
While I wait for you, I rehearse what it is I want you to know.

I want you to know my anguish and my trouble
    far more than my childhood pain.
I want you to know that I had to remember
    the wrong that was done
    and having remembered I had to confront
    and having confronted and been denied
    rejected, disinherited, slandered and mocked,
    I held on to what I knew to be true:
I did not forgive the heinous assault
    of body, mind and soul.

How could I let go of truth?
How could I forget the wounds,
    visible in part to many who knew me by day,
    and visible a hundredfold in the loneliness of night?
How could I turn my back and walk away
    from my past, my life, my self?

Who would the walking "I" be that left my self behind?

Yet there were those who told me, "You must forgive."
They warned me of eventual doom:
"No one is without sin.
You cannot be forgiven and received into heaven
    unless you first forgive the sins of those who wronged you."
And there were those who added to my burden of guilt:
    "You must forgive yourself."

As the day's heat falls away,
    as the first star twinkles in tonight's sky,
    I cry out to the land, the sea, the trees,
"No!"
I will not, I cannot, forgive myself.
As a little child badly hurt by grownups
    it was right, not wrong, for me to do
    what I did to survive.
It was right, not wrong,
    for me to be loyal to my enemies,
    for that was how I preserved life.
It was right, not wrong,
    for me to keep their secret,
    for they had far more power than I.

It was right, not wrong,

    for me to split into a dozen parts,

    for there was no other way not to be overwhelmed.

There was no other way to cling to holiness, truth, and love.

No. I have no need to forgive myself.

I have learnt instead to value, honor and respect

    all the different parts of me

    that worked together to keep me safe.

It is true that at times I have hurt other people

    as my rage spilled over on to them,

    as my fear made me withdraw from them.

But I cannot forgive myself for hurting others;

    the best I can do is ask forgiveness from them.

It is also true that I used to hate myself –

    hated my life and my powerlessness.

But I cannot forgive myself for that.

Instead I ask forgiveness from you, O Holy One,

    you who made me and gave me life,

    for in hating myself I hated what you had made.

Ah, you have been so patient with me,

    waiting for me to turn around

    to see the healing you set in my way

    and to embrace the wholeness that only faith can bring.

It is not so hard to say, "Forgive me,"

    for I have known very well your tender compassion.

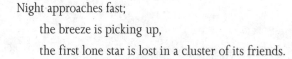

Night approaches fast;
> the breeze is picking up,
> > the first lone star is lost in a cluster of its friends.

Green leaves are darkening; I wonder where you are.

The curse of those who insist I must forgive
> in order to know heaven
> > separates me from comfort and peace.
It keeps me from what I long for most.

This night contains a contradiction:
Though the surety of your Creation
> – of earth and sky, of sea and stars –
speaks to me of connection and home,
yet the raw necessity of holding on to truth
> would estrange me, people say,
> > from you, the Creator.

My yearning this night outweighs the contradiction.
Nightfall has taken all color from the trees,
but my faith reappears green as their daytime leaves.
I offer it into the emptiness.
It is all I have.

A sudden gust of wind startles me.
Is it perhaps a sign that you are here at last?
Have you come to receive my longing and my faith
or to chastise me and cast me off?
Doubts abound when faith is strong,
> but by your power so does grace.

Even as I stand straining to sense your presence,
      a single light tears across the fabric of the night sky.
I gasp and stare wide-eyed,
      and a moment later see another bright streak,
      then another and another.
Lights are whizzing across the darkness
      chasing after each other,
      until the whole sky is sparkling
and the very universe itself dances in glee.

My former grim determination to face this night
      is wiped clear away.
I am smiling to myself,
      to the sky and to you,
      for yes, you, Holy of Holies,
      bless me with your peace.
By the gift of your Spirit
      you honor me and trust me
      to do the right thing.

You accept what I have done already
      as holy work,
      and so move me to the brink
          of laying it down,
          letting it go,
          of risking forgiveness
          and releasing into heaven
          the truth of what is past.

◇◇◇◇◇

Questions to ask ourselves

- What pressure does my faith place on me to forgive people who have hurt me?
- How comfortable am I with not forgiving?
- What would I have to do to maintain clear boundaries and expectations between myself and someone I chose not to forgive?
- What is my response when told "You must forgive yourself"?
- Is there a difference between forgiving myself and accepting myself?
- Have I ever believed I deserved to be hurt by someone older/bigger/stronger than I am?
- Are there people from whom I might one day ask forgiveness?
- How easy is it for me to ask the Creator for forgiveness?
- Can I articulate the difference between revenge and not-forgiving?

Saying yes

Offer to God a sacrifice of thanksgiving,
and pay your vows to the Most High.
Call on me in the day of trouble;
I will deliver you, and you shall glorify me.

PSALM 50:14-15

"Sacrifice" and "thanksgiving" are, at first sight, strange concepts to ponder in the context of healing from childhood abuse. A healthy reaction to these religious terms is outrage and indignation. Have we not sacrificed enough? Have we not relinquished most, if not all, of our own hopes and dreams, needs and desires, and made do with the bare minimum just to stay alive? We learnt too well to get by on too little. Long after the abuse is over we often continue to give up what we most want; maybe we have even lost the ability to know what we want. We live so close to the bottom line of simply staying alive, of acquiescing to the needs and wishes of others. We manage to survive, but not always to thrive. It is difficult to see how the notion of sacrifice relates to healing, if indeed it does.

In addition to being trained by our abuse to make sacrifices, we were also the object of someone else's (misguided) sacrifice. Instead of being steadily and consistently nurtured and treasured as children, we were used. Older people in our lives sacrificed the loving and caring relationships we ought to have had. They willingly gave them up for something dehumanizing, hurtful, and wrong. It is hard to imagine good news in sacrifice.

What about thanksgiving? Even a brief inventory of the long-term effects of child sexual abuse appears to overwhelm any possible cause for being thankful. Sometimes people who mean well, but who fail to understand the devastation in our lives, say things like, "Just think, if it had not happened you would not be such a strong person today. That's something you must be thankful for." Well, no. If "it" – and I wonder if they ever think about the evil that is embodied in that little euphemism "it" – if "it" had not happened we could have flourished so much more easily into the strong human beings we are. There is no reason to be thankful for what happened, neither directly nor indirectly. There is no gospel in the suggestion that to "make a sacrifice of thanksgiving" means to be thankful for a child's suffering.

Understandably, thanksgiving is not what first comes to mind for people who have endured abuse or for people who care for them. However, if nothing bad had ever happened, if there had been no exploitation and violation, saying "Thank you" to our Creator might possibly be the most natural thing in the world to do. If we can find a way to say "Thank you" even after what happened, an important facet of our relationship with the Holy One can be restored. Giving thanks brings back some of the dignity that was stripped away, and although it is not easy, it helps us to practice trust.

In the message of Psalm 50, the words sacrifice and thanksgiving belong together. Through the psalmist, the Creator is asking for nothing more – nor less – than a sacrifice of thanksgiving. The Holy One is not greedy for what we need for our well-being. We need to remember the pain, the betrayal, the injustice of the past, and we are not asked to sacrifice those. Rather, we are asked to pause, here and now, in the present, and – as we pause – to look around or within and find one thing that we feel thankful or happy or glad about. Nothing we find is too trivial, fleeting, or obvious, too big or little or impersonal. All that matters is that we find it. Today. Now.

Everyday kinds of things abound: a meal eaten alone or shared with friends; a familiar face on the bus; a baby's smile; a phone call from a friend; a piece of music, a song, a book, a flower, a tree, water flowing, wind blowing, waves breaking on the shore. Find something, and enjoy it. Some things like a fall of fresh snow, or a rainbow after a storm, are shared with other people. But so what? They are still there, here, now, to be enjoyed. And we can be thankful. For just a moment our eyes and ears, our heart and soul, are open to a good and freely given part of our world. We can rest with it a while. It is safe. We can let it touch us. Along with all the other real and important parts of our lives, anything that makes us smile, anything that makes us say "Yes," is also real and important.

Once we have identified something to be thankful for, we are on the way to "making a sacrifice of thanksgiving." A sacrifice is something made sacred or made holy. The emotion of thankfulness is extended by seeing the hand of the Holy One in the thing we are thankful for, whether in the company of a friend, in the surprise of snowdrops at winter's end, or in the playfulness of a child on a swing. To make a sacrifice of thanksgiving is to acknowledge the Giver of the gift, not so much in the third person as in the second person. Thank you. Thank you, Creator. Thank you, Jesus. Thank you, Spirit. Thank you, You.

The amazing thing about a sacrifice of thanksgiving is that it brings us into a closer relationship with the Holy One. Other sacrifices – the ones where we give up what we need or what is good – sometimes tend to separate us. When we say, "Thank you," we give up our separateness and reconnect with the Source of Life.

It costs nothing and it costs everything to say, "Thank you." It costs no money, no tangible thing, no piece of property, yet it costs everything because as soon as we say thank you we have said "Yes" to the Holy One. Yes, I thank you. Yes, I see you. Yes, I know you. Yes. One thank you leads to another; we begin by saying thank you for some small piece of our world, and the next thing we know we are saying thank you to the Creator for life. If we make thankfulness a habit – daily, deliberately, intentionally – we risk stumbling upon the meaning of abundant life.

We say thank you for a hug from a child, and claim our right to life.

We say thank you for the quiet at the end of a busy day, and tumble into that space in the world made entirely for us.

We say thank you anytime for life, and overcome the power of our oppressors who violated our right to a childhood filled with safety, innocence, and trust.

In this way, thanksgiving has to do with healing.

◇◇◇◇◇

After being with, listening to, and praying Psalm 50 for several days I was out walking in the mountains in North Wales, in an area I had first visited with my family. I had with me an Ordnance Survey (OS) map in case I got lost. A grid superimposed on all OS maps means it is possible to identify any place by reading the horizontal and vertical coordinates. The following is an account of what happened at OS Grid Reference 575554.

OS Grid Reference 575554

I have been a long time traveling to this holy place:
    so long I cannot tell if the joy that bubbles in my soul
    is from relief of the journey over
or from the awe-filled sanctuary that awaits.

This holy place:
    just a cleft in the mountain wall,
    sheltered from the wind,
    wide open to the wintry sun,
shining on yesterday's autumn slopes
    of brown and green and gold;
An ordinary hollow of rocks and grass,
    slate scattered on the ground;
a place to sit and rest awhile,
    eat a meal, and when the time is right,
to plan the journey on.

What makes the ordinary into beauty and truth?
(What makes the wondrous into ugliness and deceit?)

I am glad enough to be out of the wind.
Thankfully, I take off my pack
    and, travel-weary, sit down on a bare rock.
Here I am safe; nothing threatens to hurt me.
I have been a long time in coming.

Sheltered, secure, I open my bag,
    take out provisions of food and drink:
        a peanut butter sandwich and a flask of tea.
Hungry, thirsty, tired and alone,
    I barely pause to bless the meal,
    but blessed it is
for when I break the bread and pour the tea,
    suddenly all is changed.

Gone is that ancient, unanswerable question,
"Why, what is the point?"
Gone is the ache of loneliness
    that has worn my soul bare.
Gone is the terrible hunger for love
    never satisfied by bread alone.

All is transformed with the first bite of food
    and the first sip from the cup.

My question "Why?" has the answer given:
"Open your eyes and your heart, look around, see where."
This small, green, slatey place is filled with dancing;
    nothing is still;
    all is moving with the music of the heavens,
    trembling in tune with the holy,
    twinkling in the light of the Divine.

Even as I sit and marvel,
    the angels ask me to join in the dance.
All that I am falls over with forgiveness,
    yet heaven swoops down to gather me up.
Holding and supporting me,
    she breathes her strength into my limbs
    and wraps her comfort around my body,
    until I whisper
"Yes,
I would like to dance."

"Yes,"
    and as the music swells
I too am moving, trembling, twinkling.
Holiness has found me, broken and embraced me.
The bread of life and the cup of thanksgiving,
    have healed and restored me
    into communion with love.

◇◇◇◇◇

What makes the ordinary into beauty and truth?
Can it be a sandwich and a cup of tea
      on a Welsh mountainside?

The harder question is:
What makes the wondrous into ugliness and deceit?

I have been a long time traveling to this holy place.
How do I break the silence of the years
      and now tell the secrets of destruction?
Surely earth and heaven are here before me.
Judgment does not alarm me
      since righteousness is not my own.

I have known too well the sacrificial altar.
I was like Isaac on the table of his father
      but when my lamb appeared the old script was changed.
No substitute beast relieved me of my role.
Decapitated, it added to my plight.

Ah, sister Goddess, loosen my tongue and make my heart fearless,
      lest silence lock me forever within walls of terror.
Words fracture into a thousand shards
      the power of evil that all but claimed me for its own.
Words assembled into horrible truth
      shake faithfulness into the depths of my being.
Words whispered from the mountainside
      invoke heaven's storms, and the thunder of holiness.

There is no glory in the rape of a child
    tightly bound to the altar of Christ.
There is nothing sacred in the breaking of her body,
      no communion with God through the bloody lamb hung above,
      no forgiveness of sins when the ritual is over.

She knows and God knows
    the end of torture marks the beginning of rage.
Release from her father's bondage sends her soul into madness,
    and, if glory is to ever be,
    there must be no end to remembering.

I have been a long time in coming here.
Remembering, madness and rage slowed my steps.
I could no more relinquish those life-long burdens entrusted to me
    than redeem my own soul.
I have carried them many miles, many years.
Now is the right time, here is an acceptable place,
    to offer them to the Holy,
    with thanksgiving and praise.

Dear sister Goddess,
I give you the rage that saved my life,
    the remembering that was my purpose,
    the madness that kept me free.
The trust you placed in me, I now return to you,
    and find that in trusting you
I stand in the doorway to the mystery of love.

There is no other, only you,
  who brings redemption this day.
There is no other, only you,
  who is glorified forever.

◇◇◇◇◇

I have been a long time traveling to this holy place.
Before, when I even approached,
  I brought deceit as well as truth;
  I bore a mask of ugliness over beauty's face.
Before I was not ready for the reality of heaven
  revealed crystal-clear here on sacred earth.

Holy of holies,
  can you bear me up through new-found grief,
  and still help me speak my prayer, my praise?

I have been a long time in coming here,
  though I knew it dimly long ago.
Then I had a human companion,
  in my tired father, broken, yet alive,
  thankful, also, for shelter and rest.
Then our meal was much the same,
  egg sandwiches and a cup of tea.
A shadow of today's peace
  passed over as we ate.
Your dancing was disguised as a rustling in the grass,
  and the heavenly music was a murmur in the wind.
Any trust I knew was tentative at best.
I felt pity and regret, not hope or love.

What might have been was defiled, dis-graced,

    but today my prayer, through grace, is this:

    that if, in heaven, the angels are dancing

they welcome and invite my father in.

◇◇◇◇◇

Questions to ask ourselves

- What have I been forced to give up of my own needs, desires, hopes, and dreams?
- Has anyone ever suggested that my suffering is a good thing because it makes me a better, or stronger, or more understanding person? If so, how did I feel about it? How do I feel about it now?
- Am I willing to set aside a few minutes each and every day for thankfulness, a time when I do my best to get in touch with my own inner sense of gratitude?
- What am I thankful for in this moment?
- What am I thankful for when I look back over the past week? the past month? the past year?
- Am I able not just to feel thankful, but also to say "Thank you" to the Holy One? Do I then have a sense of feeling more connected, of saying "Yes"?
- Ordinary, yet specific, places are sometimes associated with moments of unexpected revelation of the Divine. Have there been such places in my life? If so, what did I experience and what changed for me?

Epilogue

A walk through an urban neighborhood

This final set of short reflections is based on a practice that since the 1980s has seen church people from many different denominations gather every Good Friday in the poorest area of Vancouver, BC, and walk together through the neighborhood commonly called the Downtown Eastside. They have stopped at twelve "stations of the cross" along the way, to read a section of the biblical narrative that describes the final suffering and death of Jesus, and to reflect on how that text addresses the concerns of people whose lives are influenced by the daily activities at each particular location. The stations include sites such as a mission church, an armaments museum, a resource center for Aboriginal women, and a courthouse. Before moving on to the next station, prayers are offered or perhaps a song is sung, to express the desire for justice and healing to come quickly to our broken world.

Child sexual abuse happens in all neighborhoods, regardless of whether they are poor, middle class, or rich. It happens wherever adults have the opportunity to take advantage of young people without being called to account for their actions.

The following reflections on the passion story from Luke's gospel (Luke 22:39 – 23:56) as it intersects the lives of those who know all too well the reality of abuse could form the basis of a group spiritual practice. As each station is considered, a group of people might discuss an equivalent place or situation in their own neighborhood. What happens there? What prayers are called for? Is there action to be taken?

Suggestions for more specific questions at the various sites:

- Dare I believe that children and young people are being sexually exploited in their homes and schools in my neighborhood, my street?
- What is my experience of telling the truth to friends, to medical professionals, or to church leaders? What sustains me when I am rejected?
- What worldly power do I threaten by my words, or actions, or silence?
- Do I pray to be disturbed as often as I pray to be comforted?
- Is it natural for me to give help? Is it natural for me to ask for help?
- Can I imagine my Creator weeping?
- Do I think it is right to expect young people to protect themselves from sexual assault? Do I blame them when they fail?
- How do I spend time completely alone except for the Holy One? What happens at such times?

The reflections do not need to be read altogether in one sitting. A summary of the text for each station is given.

◇◇◇◇◇

First station:

An apartment building

READING: LUKE 22:39-46

When Jesus prays at the Mount of Olives, he is alone. He has left his disciples a stone's throw away, expecting them to be praying too. When he left them he told them to pray that they would not know temptation. Meanwhile, Jesus himself resists the temptation to flee from what he surely knows lies ahead. He prays that the worst will not happen, and yet surrenders himself to the will of God. When an angel comes and gives him strength his prayers become more intense; "his sweat became like great drops of blood falling to the ground."

On any given evening, many of the adult residents of this apartment building will be at home after a day's work; maybe they work for a downtown law firm, or at a health clinic, or in a bank. After they have showered and changed out of work clothes into something more casual, and after they have prepared and eaten a meal, they might turn on the computer for some entertainment. Someone, somewhere in this building, will choose to go to an Internet site where they can view child pornography. Even if they know it is wrong, morally and legally, they feel sufficiently removed from the children that it hardly feels wrong most of the time. They know from oblique conversations with colleagues and friends that they are not the only ones who unwind from a day's work this way. If there is any sense of danger that they might get caught, that just adds to the excitement.

At an earlier time, and in a different place, the youngsters whose images now appear on computer screens all around the world were praying that the worst would not happen. Not this time. Please, God. Please, Universe. And if it did, if there was no other way to appease the adults, then some of them at least were able to surrender themselves to a deep inner holiness that never takes away the pain, but is a remarkable angelic presence alongside it.

O merciful Creator, we pray as Jesus taught us
    not to fall into temptation.
We pray for those who face the temptation of using child pornography.
We pray for honesty,
    for the courage to admit the wrong we know to be real.
We pray that we will resist the temptation
    to pretend there is nothing we can do to stop it.
Keep us awake to the suffering and sexual exploitation of children,
    whatever the cost.

◇◇◇◇◇

Second station:

A house with a well-kept garden and a shiny car in the driveway

READING: LUKE 22:47-53

Judas leads the authorities to Jesus and approaches Jesus to kiss him. This is the sign that will identify Jesus to the chief priests, the elders, and the temple police. Jesus challenges Judas: "Is it with a kiss that you are betraying the Son of Man?"

Inside this house – if not this exact house then another like it on this street or the next street over – a young child is wakened up at night, stripped naked, fondled, and orally raped. She or he is told never, ever to tell anyone what happens. It is a very special secret. If the secret ever gets out Mommy and Daddy won't be able to love the child anymore. That would be very sad, because right now Daddy's and Mommy's love reaches to the moon and back.

When parents treat their children this way they compound the obvious initial harm with the confusion and mixed messages about love and secrecy. A child's trust and innocence is betrayed. Just as Judas sought to protect himself by making it look as though his only feeling for Jesus was one of friendship, so do child molesters seek to protect themselves by making it look as though their only feeling for the child is love.

Holy Friend, who blesses us
> with the gift of human love and friendship,
> we pray for everyone who is betrayed
>> by parents, caregivers and friends.
Can these victims still rest in your holy friendship and love?
Can they one day heal enough to trust in human love once more?

◇◇◇◇◇

Third station:

A local high school

READING: LUKE 22:54-62

Peter follows at a distance as Jesus is taken to the high priest's house, then moves in closer and mingles with the servants of the household, waiting to see what will happen to Jesus. Three different people recognize Peter to be one of Jesus' followers. Each time they confront Peter, he denies it. After the third denial a cock crows. Jesus looks at Peter, who remembers that Jesus had predicted this just a few hours earlier. Peter is distraught and runs away.

This is a typical high school. At some point in its history something similar to this scenario has taken place. A new teacher at the school, a 23-year-old woman, has established a sexual relationship with a 15-year-old boy. He is a student at the school, though not enrolled in any of this particular teacher's classes. She thinks to herself that because she is not actually his teacher that is all right for them to be intimate.

Some students who know about the relationship are jealous of the boy. Others pretend they don't know.

Teachers at the school are divided into two camps. There are those who agree with the new teacher that since the boy is not one of her students she is doing nothing wrong. Others believe that the matter is private and none of their business. The administrative staff are too busy balancing the budget and dealing with truancy to notice what is going on.

By the time anyone wakes up and admits the teacher is guilty of sexual misconduct, the relationship is over, the teacher has moved to a different school district, and the boy – now in his twenties – is a very angry and confused young adult. Because he is no longer a minor, he is the only one who can press charges against the teacher, but he is in no shape to do that.

Holy One whose name is Truth,
    you know how many times
    vulnerable young people are denied
        the care and truthfulness they need.
You know our pretense
    and our lies that keep us from becoming involved.
We pray for ourselves,
    that we will never shirk the responsibility
        that comes with being an adult,
    the responsibility of telling the truth
    and protecting young people from exploitation
        by those in positions of power.

◇◇◇◇◇

Fourth station:

A hospital emergency department

READING: LUKE 22:63-65

After Jesus was captured he was mocked, beaten, and blindfolded. They kept asking him, "Prophesy! Who is it that struck you?"

People who were abused as children often grow up with unresolved feelings of shame, guilt, anger, self-loathing, and despair. It is not uncommon for them to feel suicidal, especially if they are living without the support of good friends. If they harm themselves, they might end up in the emergency department of their local hospital.

In many hospitals the staff are caring, competent and compassionate people, but occasionally a patient who has attempted suicide is treated poorly. The person is asked: "How stupid can you be? Why did you do it? Can't you think of any other way to get attention?" And if it is not the first suicide attempt, he or she might overhear a caregiver say, "You'd think they would get it right one of these times and actually do themselves in, once and for all."

Patients are subjected to rough handling during stomach pumping. If they are perceived to be violent they are put in restraints. The sensitivity shown that will open up a conversation about the underlying distress is not always shown.

When anyone desperate enough to attempt to take their own life is bullied by people who are supposed to care, they share in the mockery that Jesus faced at the hands of his captors.

Dear Holy Companion, we pray for understanding
    to replace ignorance,
    and for an end to the taunting of people in despair.
We pray for compassion
    to overflow the hearts of those
        who care for people
        who see death as the only way out of pain.
We pray for tenderness and love
    to be showered like gentle healing rain
    on those who need it most.

◇◇◇◇◇

Fifth station:

A church

READING: LUKE 22:66-71

The religious authorities question Jesus about his true identity. They want to trap him into saying he is the Messiah, but he refuses to say, knowing that they will not believe. When asked if he is the Son of God, he turns their question around and replies, "You say that I am." They seize this answer as a blasphemous admission.

A parishioner goes to her priest to talk to him about having been sexually abused as a child, by a priest in a different parish. The priest would rather not hear what she has to say. He does not want to think about the steps he ought to take next. So he counsels her to pray for help in forgiving the abusive priest; he counsels her to ask for forgiveness for herself; and he strongly urges her to leave the incident in the past and not talk about it to anyone else. The woman who, out of concern for her church, opened herself to give the gift of truth is silenced. Again.

Holy One, too often your church says it seeks truth,
> but doesn't like what it finds.

Your church prays for justice,
> but won't help it happen.

Your church proclaims your peace,
> but it is nothing except empty talk.

May your church yet be redeemed,
> so that those who come to it with truth,
> seeking justice and peace,
> may be truly honored.

◇◇◇◇◇

Sixth station:

A women's resource center

READING: LUKE 23:1-5

Jesus is taken from the religious authorities to be questioned by Pilate and Herod, who are representatives of the secular, Roman authorities. At first Pilate says he can find no reason to charge Jesus, but the religious leaders insist that he is a rabble rouser. When Herod takes over the questioning, Jesus remains silent. Herod then treats Jesus with contempt, mocking him, and dressing him in royal finery. He sends him back to Pilate to decide what to do. Herod and Pilate who were formerly enemies become friends because of Jesus; both perceive him as a threat to the Roman state.

Women's resource centers have been established in many towns and cities as places where women can go to feel safe. Many of the people who visit the centers are seeking to break out of a cycle of violence in their lives. Being trapped in violence often began with early childhood experiences of physical and/or sexual assault. Gradually, with the support of places such as women's centers, women learn to recognize patterns of violence and confront the people responsible. They gain control of their own lives, and develop skills that help them become independent of abusive partners. The legacy of an abusive childhood is transformed from weakness into power.

But what a threat to the status quo of society! The empowerment of women to be fully themselves instead of what patriarchy had created them to be is a radical act indeed. No wonder that from time to time governments undermine the work of women's centers by withdrawing funding. Politicians at all levels of government use the argument that women are safe these days, that the police are there for them whenever necessary, that the healthcare system is enough to help them deal with any fallout from childhood abuse.

O Creator, who knows both strength and weakness,
    who has promised to bring down the mighty and raise up the weak,
    now is the time to confront those who misuse power
        because of their own fears.
Now is the time to align the work of governments
    with the desires of the needy.
Now is the time for a grand celebration
    of women working together to end all forms of violence.
Now is not a time for silence but for shouting out!

◇◇◇◇◇

Seventh station:

A hospital psychiatric ward

READING: LUKE 23:13-25

Pilate brings Jesus back to the people, saying that he finds him innocent of the charges they had laid. He will have him flogged and then released. But the crowd shouts for Jesus to be crucified. Twice more Pilate says he can find nothing for which Jesus deserves to be killed. But the crowd is insistent and Pilate eventually gives in to them, and hands Jesus over to be crucified.

In our society adults who are troubled by experiences of childhood sexual abuse sometimes are labeled mentally ill. Perhaps they are deeply depressed, or unable to sleep without terrifying nightmares. Perhaps their trust in other people is so diminished they show signs of paranoia. Perhaps their daily anxiety level is so high they are unable to hold down a job.

When such people are hospitalized, careful medical intervention can initiate healing. However, at other times, confinement in a psychiatric ward can mean being sentenced to isolation, heavy sedation, or invasive electric shock treatment – or a combination of all three.

There is much wrong with a society that hands over vulnerable people to institutions where their right to proper health care is ignored, and where their dignity is stripped away. When we store hurting people in warehouses, we think we are free of them. We have put them out of sight; we can forget about them and get on with life as though they didn't exist, and as though their profound pain could be countered by pills, and straitjackets, and body-wrenching voltages.

Holy and disturbing Spirit,
    just as Jesus' contemporaries did not know what to think of him,
    or how to respond to his teaching,
we do not know what to think of the mentally ill,
    or how to respond to their situation.
Instead of sentencing them to a life not worth living
    and sentencing ourselves to continued ignorance,
we pray for them and us, that we might yet learn how to love.
We pray to know your disturbance rather than your absence.

◇◇◇◇◇

Eighth station:

A detox center

READING: LUKE 23:26

*As they led Jesus away, they seized a Roman man, Simon of Cyrene, who was
coming from the country, and they laid the cross on him, and made him carry
it behind Jesus.*

In being sentenced to die, Jesus is a victim of a political system run by people
who needed to hold on to power. They saw him as a threat to their power.

Jesus is expected to carry his own cross to the place where executions
were carried out, but after the ordeal of the last 24 hours, including trials and
beatings, he is simply too weak and collapses under the weight of his cross.
Simon of Cyrene might not have had anything to do with Jesus prior to being
enlisted to carry his cross for him, but he was forced to help.

Children who suffer sexual abuse are also victims of people who need to
hold on to power. In the absence of sufficient help to deal with having been
abused, people will often turn to alcohol or drugs as a way to cope. Although
this might relieve symptoms in the short term, eventually the initial harm
inflicted in childhood will be exacerbated by the problems of addiction.

The staff at a detox center are like Simon of Cyrene – they take care of the
immediate needs of those they serve. They do what they can, accompanying
the wounded on their journey to break the power of addiction. This first step
needs to happen before people can heal properly from child sexual abuse.

Vulnerable One, you come to us in the needy, the despised, and the weak.
Give us the grace of Simon
    to accompany those who need us most.
Give us the humility to ask for help
    when we ourselves are empty of power.

◇◇◇◇◇

Ninth station:

A bus station

READING: LUKE 23:27-31

The women who follow Jesus to the place where he is to be crucified are over-whelmed with grief. Jesus tells them not to weep for him, but for themselves and their children. Worse days lie ahead. A time is coming when it will be better for women not to become mothers, when they will welcome their own destruction by the very earth.

Here and there signs prove society is waking up to the widespread nature of childhood sexual abuse. Advertisements inside city buses inform riders where they can get help if they have suffered abuse. There are three different posters – one for men, one for women, and one for children. Each has a picture of a typical "survivor"; they look like you or me. They could be our neighbors, or the children who we see playing in the park. They are ordinary people. Each poster gives the name of a counseling agency and the phone number of the appropriate help-line.

True: not all buses display these ads, and when they do it is only for about two weeks at a time. It is a beginning, but only that. More has yet to be acknowledged.

Are we bold enough to stay with the pain of sexual abuse, to be open to knowing the full extent of it, to meet the challenge of more and more people coming forward to press charges against family members, teachers, clergy, police officers, etc.? Are we ready for the pain and grief yet to be unleashed? Are we ready for the worse days that lie ahead?

Holy Judge, we weep for victims of abuse,
    whatever their age or gender or religion or race.
We weep for ourselves
    in our helplessness to bring an instant cure
        to those who suffer.
We weep for the generations
    who will continue to live under the terrible shadow
        of our secrecy and lies,
        of our denial and betrayal.
Will you, our Judge, also be our Hope?

◇◇◇◇◇

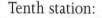

Tenth station:

A pre-school

READING: LUKE 23:32-43

When Jesus is crucified along with two criminals, one on his left, the other on his right, he prays for his executors: "Father, forgive them, for they do not know what they are doing." Meanwhile, some people stand quietly by, watching. Others scoff at Jesus, saying "Let him save himself." One of the criminals voices a similar sentiment: "Are you not the Messiah? Save yourself and us!" But the other one admits he is a criminal and asks Jesus to remember him when he enters his kingdom.

For at least the last decade, all children who attend pre-school in Canada have been taught the importance of keeping themselves safe. They are told never to speak to strangers, not to take candies from someone they don't know, not to get into a car unless they know the driver. They are told about bad touching, and the importance of not keeping secrets.

Given the prevalence of child abuse in our society it is imperative we do whatever we can to protect youngsters. Parents, social workers, teachers, police officers, and religious ministers are all supportive of "Keep Safe" programs.

Yet is this not also a horrifying reflection of who we are as a society? What does it mean that we tell – even expect and demand – innocent three- and four-year-olds to protect themselves from adults? Are little children supposed to save themselves? If only they could, then perhaps we would feel saved too. We would feel we had solved our problem of having child molesters living in every community.

Every time we teach another youngster how to keep himself or herself safe, we do so because of a criminal element in our society. The more we put the onus on the child for preventing criminal behavior, the less responsibility we take for addressing the root cause. The parallel between telling Jesus to save himself from his suffering, and telling little children to save themselves from theirs, is dis-comforting.

O Source of Power and Transformation,
    help us to see the injustice
    the insanity
    of having to train vulnerable, little children to negate the evil
        perpetrated by the guilty and the powerful.
Help us recognize our own complicity
    and our own power.
Turn us around to a right way of thinking and acting
    that ushers in your beautiful reign
        of righteousness and peace.

◇◇◇◇◇

Eleventh station:

A secluded place, out-of-doors

READING: LUKE 23:44-49

At the moment of Jesus' death, we glimpse a holy intimacy when he cries out and says, "Father, into your hands I commend my spirit." Although there are people around watching — the centurion, the crowds, the women, and other acquaintances standing at a distance — Jesus is deserted by the very people he came to love. He throws himself back into the hands of the Creator.

As a little child I sometimes used to find a patch of tall grass where I could crouch down so that I was out of sight of anyone who might pass by. More importantly, they were out of sight of me. My immediate physical surroundings supported me in my aloneness. They were a true reflection of my emotional reality: silenced, friendless, and desolate concerning the enormous suffering and weight of nighttime victimization, torture, and rape. There in the grass I would nestle down, finding for myself a temporary safe place where I could cry out all my torment and rage, all my pain and confusion. So it was that the damp earth beneath me, and the gray sky above, the scratchy stalks of grass rustling with the wind, all cradled my body and received my spirit. Holiness was incarnate once again.

O Great Creator and friend of little children
    when there is no other hope
    you come to us in earth and sky
    to receive us with our pain and longing.
You bear the weight of our sadness,
    absorb the desperation of our screams,
    hold us close against your body.
You are our only refuge;
you give us respite from betrayal and assault.
We rest in your holy presence.

◇◇◇◇◇

Twelfth station:

A street-youth drop-in center

READING: LUKE 23:50-56

There was a good and righteous man named Joseph, from Arimathea, who though a member of the council, had not agreed to their plan and action. He asked Pilate for Jesus' body, and took it down, wrapped it in a cloth, and laid it in a rock-hewn tomb. The women who saw him do this came back later with spices and ointments.

Seventy percent of the street youth who come to this drop-in center were abused in their family home. At the center they have a locker for all their worldly belongings; they are given a nutritious meal; their pets – their trusted companions – are welcome. The center is a place of respite from the rain, from the hot sun, from the concrete sidewalks, and from the stares or turned heads of passers-by. What the center is not, is a cure. Its stated mission is harm reduction. All of the staff were street-involved themselves at one time, as were many of the volunteers.

Joseph of Arimathea was a good man, who dared to disagree with the other members of the council who helped to condemn Jesus. He did what he could to show respect to Jesus, even if he couldn't prevent his death. Likewise, the people who look after the street youth show caring and honor to the full extent of their ability. They take a stand against the dominant voice that says young people exaggerate their problems, that they ought to return home, be grateful, get an education, and make a contribution to society.

Ah, Holy One,
> who are we to judge hurting children
> who choose to live rough on our city streets?
Open our hearts and minds to their anguish,
> their needs, their hopes and fears and dreams.
Open our hands in compassion.
Hew out of the rigid ideas
> and the fixed routines of our lives
an emptiness that can be a place of welcome and rest.

◇◇◇◇◇

Suggestions for further reading

This compilation includes the references made to other authors, as well as several other publications relevant to the intersection of spirituality and childhood sexual abuse.

Bray, Madge.
Poppies on the Rubbish Heap.
Sexual Abuse: The Child's Voice.
Edinburgh: Canongate Press, 1991.

Campbell, Beatrix.
Unofficial Secrets.
London: Virago, 1988.

Cashman, Hilary.
Christianity and Child Sexual Abuse.
London: SPCK, 1993.

Chödrön, Pema.
The Places that Scare You:
A Guide to Fearlessness in Difficult Times.
Boston: Shambhala, 2002.

Cummings, Louise.
Eyes Wide Open.
Kelowna, BC: Wood Lake Books,
1994.

Eliot, T. S.
Four Quartets.
London: Faber and Faber, 1944.

Forest, Heather.
Wisdom Tales From Around the World.
Little Rock, AR: August House Inc.,
1996.

ed. Marie M. Fortune.
Journal of Religion and Abuse.
Binghampton, NY: The Haworth Press
Inc. Published quarterly since 1999.

Gutierrez, Gustavo.
On Job:
God-Talk and the Suffering of the Innocent.
Maryknoll, NY: Orbis Books, 1987.

Keenan, Brian.
An Evil Cradling.
London: Vintage, 1993.

Linn, Dennis, Sheila Fabricant Linn
and Matthew Linn, S. J.
Don't Forgive Too Soon:
Extending the Two Hands That Heal.
Mahwah, NJ: Paulist Press, 1997.

Michaels, Anne.
Fugitive Pieces.
Toronto: McClelland and Stewart Inc.,
1996.

Miller, Alice.
Thou Shalt Not Be Aware:
Society's Betrayal of the Child.
Trans. Hildegarde and Hunter
Hannum. New York: Meridian, 1984.

Olsen, Sylvia
with Rita Morris and Ann Sam.
No Time to Say Goodbye: Children's Stories
of Kuper Island Residential School.
Vancouver: Sono Nis Press, 2001.

Proulx, Annie.
The Shipping News.
New York: Simon and Schuster Inc.,
1993.

Thomas, R. S.
The Kingdom in Collected Poems,
1945 – 1990.
London: Phoenix, 2000.

Walker, Alice.
The Color Purple.
New York: Pocket Books, 1982.

Wiesel, Elie.
Night.
Trans. Stella Rodway.
New York: Avon Books, 1960.

Northstone Publishing

Northstone Publishing is committed to supporting
and encouraging an emerging form of
Christianity, which recognizes that faith must
evolve with life, and which, at the same time, is
rooted in ancient Christian tradition.

Far from being superficial or trendy, this
commitment is grounded in the Bible (Christian
scripture) and requires us to be dedicated to
spiritual practice and faithful to living out our
values in the world.

We are open and inclusive, and honor the
perennial wisdom and truth contained in all of
the world's enduring religions. We affirm the
equality of the sexes and the godliness of people
of all ages, races, and nationalities. We believe
that the natural world is a sacred part of creation
and needs to be treated as such. We emphasize
the process of transformation rather than
adherence to doctrine or belief.

where spirituality and real life meet

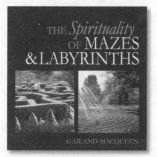
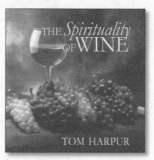